THIS SACRED SPACE

THIS SACRED SPACE

MARK PERRY

Drama Circle
P.O. Box 3844
Chapel Hill, NC 27515 USA

Email: info@dramacircle.org
Website: www.dramacircle.org

Front and Back Images are taken from the UNC Department of Dramatic Art's 2024 production of *The Seagull.* Photos by HuthPhoto.

Book 2 of the 19 X 19 CHALLENGE

This Sacred Space: Considerations on the Practice of Theatre

ISBN: 978-1-953219-02-2
Library of Congress Control Number: Pending

26 27 28 29 30 31 10 9 8 7 6 5 4 3 2 1

To my students and young colleagues

Each generation holds
the requisite energy to heal.
But the remedy cannot be broadcast,
only shared heart to heart

Table of Contents

Preface & Acknowledgment

I offer this small book as a contribution to the ongoing dialogue among theatre folk as to the direction to incline our art. All the elements I speak of, any suggestions I make, these are already out there to some greater or lesser degree in the theatre world. I am myself seeking to synthesize and understand these ideas, and I would hope to encourage others, especially young practitioners, along a conscientious path. These understandings are just as likely to be gained in classrooms and black box theatres as on professional stages. But sacred space is sacred space, just as the ocean is held in the drop.

My gratitude goes to my wife, Azi, and to my parents, and to all my circles and communities. Ever nearer, ever dearer.

MP

April 2026

1

Introduction

Recently, my wife Azi and I drove a van full of middle-schoolers over to a local middle school to watch a girls' basketball game. We came to see Esther* play. She's a sharp, caring and funny sixth grader who had made the team and gone out of her way a couple of times to remind her junior youth group of their game schedule. So we arranged to come on this particular Thursday afternoon when they were playing another local school. Azi and I have been serving in Esther's community for years working with kids and their families through a local initiative.

I had forgotten how loud a school gymnasium can get, especially when there are more cheerleaders than there are players. We were sitting down just as the home team's J.V. squad entered, jogging in to boisterous cheering. I was surprised to see Esther not with them. They fell into a passing drill, and then I noticed Esther and maybe 4 or 5 other girls sitting down on the bench, at the other end away from the coach. These girls didn't even have a team shirt, but were

---

* Names are changed throughout the book … except when they're not.

wearing some scrubby, leftover clothes they found lying in a pile in some stinky locker.

I know this is not true, but indignation can grip my imagination sometimes. I thought back to my days as a bench warmer for my 9th grade basketball team—at least we had the same shirts as the kids who played. The moment had stirred up in me a host of dormant feelings, as this seemed to typify everything I wanted to get away from in this competition-focused, scarcity-minded society, which exalts a perceived elite, while everyone else grovels and grumbles for scraps.

The kids we had brought from Esther's neighborhood to watch the game also go to this same school. Watching them settle into the bleachers, I could sense the varying degrees of belonging they felt here. These kids live in Section 8 public housing and represent mostly immigrant and all racial minority households. They live in a historically redlined complex separated from shopping by a 4-lane highway, where pedestrians have lost their lives trying to cross. They are situated on the flooding end of a creek, and when they are displaced by flooding, the town does not heed their families' modest requests. Many of the parents have to work at night and sleep in the day, and so the kids miss out on quality time with them. Despite all this, these kids don't see themselves as victims. No, they have been arising in service to others, developing their sense of community, of collaboration, and of care. They think about their neighbors; they advocate for those less fortunate; they share what they have; they sacrifice to uplift. They rejuvenate your hope for humanity.

So now the game against the rival middle school has started, and I look and I see Esther and the other kids down the end of the bench and I don't see grumbling and groveling. No, these kids have set aside the quiet humiliation of exclusion and they kindheartedly cheer on their teammates. And I'm reminded of the resilience of goodness. I'm reminded how much we long to be part of a team, to lose ourselves in the spirit of togetherness and collective endeavor.

On the weekend, we work with these kids to encourage that spirit, and we see the effect of a few hours investment. But then they go to school, and despite the best intentions of teachers, administrators, and coaches—for scarcity seems baked into the very bricks—the kids breathe in and choke on and swallow the noxious lessons of the brute philosophy of survival of the fittest. By the end of the week, we see the results. They're dispirited, distracted, or calloused. And so we begin the work again.

Abundance is the optimal state of a mind in full health. The virus of scarcity, however, is wickedly contagious.

Anyway, I pushed past the moment and put in some ear plugs, and Azi and I started cheering along with everyone else even though we didn't know the girls on the court. I found myself cheering for whoever made a good shot or a good play on either team. I mean, this isn't the UNC-Duke game. Later, I did learn later that Esther had played for 5 minutes before we arrived in some exhibition they call the squab league, or the scrubs or whatever. Crumbs for the noble-hearted.*

* I do understand the value of competition in awakening excellence and a sense of striving.

It was in middle school—or junior high, as we called it—where I found theatre. Or I should say where theatre crashed down on me like a revelation.

It was a March evening, and I came in from the New Hampshire cold to join the audience waiting for the start of the EAJHS production of *My Fair Lady.* It was held in our school cafetorium. All the lunchroom tables had been folded up and pushed aside and folding chairs placed out in "theatre" style facing away from the kitchen and towards the stage end. I found a seat pretty far back from the stage, indeed not far from where pizza rectangles and tater tots had been served some hours before, and indeed the same area where I had struggled to find people to sit with who might not make fun of me for my paper bag lunch with the shamefully healthy sandwich that included whole grain bread and (sigh) bean sprouts, people who would not convulsively scoff at my discount brand boots that were definitely too shiny and not quite the right stitching to pass for Timberlands.

This was the same cafetorium where, months before at our first school dance, James Bowden and I had arrived dressed up—he in a coat and tie, me with nice pants and a sweater—only to discover we had woefully misread the situation with school dances. Having filed in amongst the scores of kids wearing ripped jeans and Ozzy Osborne or Iron Maiden t-shirts, James and I tried and failed to recede into the walls as the mockery cackled forth. Where did these kids get the memo? And what mineral from the New England granite shelf seeped into the water and gave them the stamina to constantly make fun of anyone who veered even slightly from the norm?

So there I sat in this familiar, yet alienating space, in this den of perpetual micro-traumas. The curtain that was always closed during lunch now rippled with the activity happening behind it. A bunch of my classmates were involved—some were friends, although in 7th grade, that distinction was tenuous, as alliances and allegiances shifted frequently. But I knew Bob McGarity was in it, and Kerri Ripley—who of course I had a crush on. Also Mark D'Angelo, who was a good singer, and Dan Cantor, who was already a baritone in 7th grade.

The 3-piece pit band started up the overture, and soon the curtain opened, and the show was launched. Henry Higgins was played by 8th grader Eric Saville, who was tall, a bit stiff, and highly cerebral, and he was doing a noble job of reciting what was far too many lines for a 14-year-old to memorize. I didn't know the 8th grade girl playing Eliza Doolittle, but I think her name was Kristen. Most of my classmates were in the Tottenham Court crowd, and they were having a jubilant time singing and dancing and with no apparent fear of mockery!

This story was so utterly different than the everyday circumstances of our adolescent lives in the land of Live Free or Die, so it took me a while to orient myself in it. But as I did, a revelation was dawning on me. It was like the roof was lifting up or light was streaming down, but the space had categorically transformed.

What was this conceit of collective imagination that had somehow opened a portal to this shared psychic experience? For one thing, all were on the same team in this endeavor.

Everyone in the cast and crew—cooler kids, nerds, unpopular kids—all were working toward a common end and not against each other for some capricious victory. In the audience were more people—including some very cool kids!—who were cheering them on as well.

Here it was. A solution to the problem that had vexed me. Collaboration. Unified action. No winners, no losers. Everyone raised up through collective enterprise. A circle that encompassed all, not an arena for combat. The lion and the lamb lain down together.

Now this production may not have been memorable for others in the audience. Some adults may have even been a little put-out by having to sit through a 2 1/2-hour musical put on by orange-faced pubescents singing in Cockney accents. But that is not the show I remember. I remember my friends fusing in a moment of rare harmonization in what was otherwise to me a largely dissonant world.

And to put a finer point on it: it was not the performances or the story, or the music, or the applause, or any technical element that caught my wonder. It was the transformation of the space and the effect it had on the people within it. That was the magic.

8th grade would follow, and I auditioned for the school musical, got a lead role, and got to experience the exhilaration of the other side of that shared psychic experience. I was hooked.

My director on that show was Mr. Jordan, who was a history teacher in the school. In 9th grade, Mr. Jordan would be the coach of the basketball team on which I warmed the bench. Some time after that basketball season had finished, Mr. Jordan and I were walking together and he casually said, "You know, you don't need to play basketball."

Now this might have sounded like a slight coming from someone else. I had had an extended career of mediocre achievement involving many sports since first grade. I was used to the slights, even from coaches. But that's not what this was.

"You're good at theatre," he continued. "That's what you should focus on."

It wasn't a very long conversation, but it stands out from my younger years as a time when I felt seen and cared for by a male figure in my life. I took the hint—or the permission, rather, and I never tried out for another sports team again. Instead, I performed in every play our high school did. And I rode that dream to college, where I majored in theatre arts. I started with acting, then leaned into directing, found a niche in composing music for non-musicals, and then decided playwriting was my calling. I went to grad school for playwriting, practiced the craft for a few years, and got a part-time job teaching it at a respected university. That job unfolded into a career teaching theatre, where my students treat me with respect and my colleagues treat me as a trusted colleague. And yet…

Why do I feel like I'm still on the bench?

Like I've practiced for 30 years, but never really played. Yes, I've had some productions of my plays, including some profound and meaningful experiences. I've also faced disappointment after disappointment, eventually leading to such a deep disillusionment I determined for my own wellbeing I should not continue. I basically stopped writing for a couple of years. I have felt outside, not only the arena of professional success, but of the circle of those who may legitimately call themselves theatre artists.

How is it that the sacred task that called out to me in a junior high cafetorium, that led me through so many difficult days of self-questioning, that has continued to reveal itself to me over the years in small insights and gob-smacking revelations, how is it that I could feel I don't belong in that space?

I am not alone in this. Many of us who love and practice this art feel, to a greater or lesser extent, on the outside of the circle. Why is this? Is this thing we love rejecting us? Is it inevitable that a theatre artist must live a life filled with rejection and self-doubt? Then again, is it the art rejecting us or some other voice that we are mistaking for the art? How much of that feeling is coming from the institution? How much of it is internalized? Is this our unweeded garden grown to seed, and can we hope to revive it? How do we find our place back in the circle?

The goal of this little book, this meditation, is to pursue these questions for potential answers and perhaps for the deeper questions they lead to, and from this, I would hope to gain some perspective to restore ourselves to our right place inside theatre's embrace.

Part One

Abundance

2

This Sacred Space

There's something that happens when we walk into an empty theatre.

There's a hush. Like a whispered welcome. It's hard to account for it simply in terms of architecture. Is it something that just some of us are attuned to?

It is in some ways like entering a temple, or a cathedral or mosque. There is a shift we experience walking in, which makes us pause and take in not just the adornment, but the openness. This openness is paradoxical in effect, for it feels like an invitation to look within.

In ways a theatre is also different than a house of worship. Less weight, less obligation. Those spaces may be illuminated with a very specific light, may resonate with a distinct subaural hymn. They host a certain repertoire, sometimes with a centuries-long run.

The theatre is more pliant, receptive to every directive and to all flights of fancy. Any story can be told there. It's like a friend that's up for anything! Sometimes you sail to the moon, sometimes you stall and sputter, sometimes you crash and burn, but soon enough, all remnants of that last show are struck. Sets come down, the floor is swept, lights returned, cables coiled, curtains restored. And our malleable friend is back, ready for another adventure.

Theatre is our temple for story.

I've named this book *This Sacred Space.*

"This" indicates how close it is, right before us, and ours whenever we want it.

"Space" means an essential element is that our bodies—or, if you will, our embodied spirits—are in presence with one another, breathing the same air, ready to connect on all those hidden levels we don't quite understand yet.

"Sacred" is the tricky word here, with its religious connotations, and I want to take care in respecting what angle the reader may be coming from. How do we use a term like sacred or holy without drawing a circle that excludes some people? And yet how do we frame the rarefied effect this art has shown us without referencing its mystical nature?

Theatre is not just an empty space, but a threshold. A portal where we access something sublime, an energy, what feels like living, purifying, beckoning presence. In another age, we might have called it a Muse. Whatever is there has a power. And we should take care how we approach it.

A Welcoming Environment

My humble suggestion: let our first rule of approach in tending to this sacred space be to welcome all and not to limit who may enter. Let's strive for universal accessibility to the theatre. This includes all avenues to the art form from makers to partakers, from backstage to the back row, whatever age or origin, whatever level of capacity or engagement.

Let our welcome be like warm water the newly arrived one may enter. They may then feel free to strip off the outer garments of hesitancy and anxiety and doubt, and they may enter this pool and become immersed in and contribute to the warmth of our company. Indeed, if all are not welcome, what claim to sacredness can we make, since the Sacred is that which beckons all?

In another time and age, we might have had a system where you had to prove your worth, or pay your dues, or face some other form of patriarchal hazing that really has so little value left in it. Let us cease from gatekeeping. Let us refrain from letting power or position dictate terms. Such is desecration.[†]

Yes, theatre has rules and best practices, and there are behaviors that will get you ushered out of the space. But let it be a first principle of our art that all are welcome and that they do not have to change any fundamental aspect of their person or identity—neither stoop, nor strain—to enter.

Now if we have been trained in a theatre practice that is exclusive or unwelcoming, a basic step we can take is to acknowledge that many of our impulses and behaviors may be guided unconsciously by outmoded standards of hierarchy and mainstream cultural hegemony. We can then set ourselves the task of bending to the new. Like the tender seedling just breaking from the dirt, or like the craggy, gnarled limb's

† I speak not of commercial theatre. I've never known that life. Let the people who work there wrestle with these ideas.

emerging green shoot, let us incline to the light of this day. And not to a memory of where light once was. We can learn how to draw our circle such that it includes all.

The circle is sacred. The circle is not defined by what is in the center. It is defined by the myriad points that make up its circumference. Or in another framing, a circle is a line moving out in all directions at once.

One of the ways I have learned to judge the health of a group dynamic is to look at how that group responds when a new person enters the space. First, is that person acknowledged? Are they welcomed? Even if they arrive late? Not just by the person "in charge", but by the collective? There are certainly situations where sensitive conversations or intense creative work must not be disturbed with latecomers interrupting the process, but what about when that is not the case?

For example, if we are in a class or rehearsal and we are all sitting in a circle in discussion, and someone walks in, do we widen the circle to allow the person to join? Does someone go and get a chair or make room next to themselves? Or do we avoid eye contact with that person or give them the stink eye for breaking the code of punctuality? Do they have to tap someone on the shoulder to make room or, worse yet, do they sit outside the circle?

The circle is sacred, but only inasmuch as we are flexible in responding to the requirements of sacredness as they present themselves in the moment. How attentive we are to the newcomer is a vital sign of our connection to sacredness. This is a touchstone. There is no mistaking it.

A Concentrated Environment

If our first attribute of sacred space is a spirit of openness and welcome, the second may well be an intensity of concentration that invites alchemy and *enthousiasmos* and shuns interruption and distraction. This is the environment where ritual and silence may probe our depths, or where boisterous dance and primal shout may free us from our bonds. This is how we transcend and transform.

We have no art if we have no concentration. Like all crafts, refinement comes in the attentive hours spent in practice. This is a well understood concept in the theatre and our training and rehearsal standards reinforce this. If concentration itself is a greater struggle in our age, its necessity is all the more appreciated.

You may notice that these two primary principles I am advocating stand in some opposition to one another. Like water and fire, openness and concentration are indispensable elements of our art that must be harmonized, or else one may threaten the other. There is no formula, but mindfulness will be key in negotiating the two. Fire and water can coexist—a candle floating on still water.

My Experience

There are many countries and many communities around the world that show remarkable hospitality. My native land is not one of them. I am so grateful I was taught openness and welcome living among two peoples in my life: the people of Botswana for 6 months in my youth and then decades spent with my Iranian friends and (later) family. These were the two that taught me what it felt like to be truly and <u>unconditionally</u>

welcomed. And I came to recognize that feeling as sacred, and I have striven to practice it. As a born-and-bred Yankee, however, I will always speak that language with an accent.

Intensity of concentration I learned in my artistic training. Acting, voice, and movement teachers were key there. The finest directors facilitated some of the quietest rehearsals, allowing the actors' imaginations to relax and sink into given circumstances, to plumb depths of grief or burst out with indignant rage. This is tender work; you can't have people clomping in and out indiscriminately. There are certainly shows where the audience should be talking back and hooting and hollering. But in *Death of a Salesman*'s penultimate scene, I didn't appreciate the two folks behind me laughing and speaking in their Slavic tongue.

I admit: I'm among the theatre people with a pet peeve for those who don't respect theatre etiquette. The khesh-khesh of the polypropylene-aluminum bag, the chomp-chomp of the chips, and the pound-pound throbbing in my head will start to drown out the inner philosopher who counsels it's not that important in the vast scheme of things.

Yes, theatre etiquette needs reinforcement. Yes, those who assume it is similar to cinema etiquette are not quite correct. Yes, the greatest stage work happens when we as an audience are enthralled. But my first priority in restoring our sacred space will be trying to make sure that new folks, even those who transgress our traditions, enjoy themselves and are eager to come back.

As Chekhov reminds us in one of his stories: *"Good breeding is shown, not by not upsetting the sauce, but by not noticing it when somebody else does."*

3

A Sense of Belonging

There are thousands of determined theatre administrators in the U.S. alone striving and struggling to widen the net and broaden their theatres' audience. This is challenging in an era with the older subscriber base dying off and younger patrons tending to be non-committal. How do we welcome in those who hesitate to come? Are we just in an era of fading interest in our art form? Perhaps it depends on who we mean when we say "we." Chinese theatre audiences are full of young people eager for social interaction and meaningful emotional engagement. "The sun rises and the sun sets, and hurries back to where it rises."

Opening up to audience is one area where we practice welcome, but what about among ourselves? If the theatre is a sacred space, what about the rehearsal room? What about auditions? Welcome and hospitality are not for the guest alone. Kindness and service are only amplified when we know and care for people. Let us not be like those families who are boisterously welcoming to the visitor, but neglectful of the children.

Do we greet one another when we enter and say goodbye when we leave? Throughout, collegiality and respect are fundamental and independent of position or prominence. The work can be quite emotional, quite straining. So we check in with one another; we are attentive to one another's moods and changes. We take breaks, we offer hugs or we offer space, depending on the need. We allow people the flow of their feelings, but the mood of the room is one of attentiveness and care. And lightness. Plants thrive in light; creative collaboration thrives in lightness.

We might think such an environment depends on the director and stage management, but perhaps this responsibility can be lightened by spreading it out among the company generally. The theatre itself may be owned by others, the director and producers may run the show, but sacred space is communally created. All may contribute to a welcoming and hospitable atmosphere, but first we must feel like we are home, like we belong.

If you're involved in a show, ask yourself: do I feel I belong here in this space? This is not a theoretical question. It is practical. There are feelings we associate with belonging, certain sensations in our body, certain emotions. For example, is our anxiety amplified in the space? Or is it eased? Am I trying to please someone here? That may mean that I believe this is their space and not mine. Do I feel I need to prove myself to be worthy of this space?

In certain theatre environments, the hierarchy of the space is emphasized. And there is a sense that agency flows from the director to the stage manager and into the actors and into the designers and to crew members or to admin staff. This is an old, outmoded framework.

In an even older framework, there's a group of fifty dancers and worshipers, moving in sync, chanting in sync, delighting in the ritual repetition of their divine story. Out of enthusiasm, one jumps apart, takes on a role and begins a dialogue, voicing the language of the god, while the chorus responds in kind, until the dialogue is done and the individual gives up the role, returns to the group, and they continue their procession. Let us not emphasize our roles in the sacred task but rather delight in the specific ways we participate. Every point on the circle has a different view, and all are valuable.

An Offering, Not an Obligation

A welcoming space can be assisted with certain material inducements. For example, having beverages and refreshments available is a way to help. At the very least water, but tea and coffee are universally understood as extensions of hospitality. One may venture into baked goods, but not every rehearsal can or should be a potluck dinner or catered affair. Providing too much can be counterproductive, as it may establish a pattern that reinforces passivity among those who otherwise might occasionally contribute a pan of brownies or a pot of soup from time to time. For example, if the stage manager or director are always providing refreshments, the rest of the company loses the sense that they may participate. The greater goal is an environment where all take ownership of the space and consider how they might contribute.

Hospitality can be tricky when it starts to feel transactional. "I will bring the refreshments this time if you do it next time."

This is okay to an extent, but when generosity or sacrifice is somehow turned to obligation, it loses some of its sweetness. However a company wishes to do this is of course up to them, but I know I feel most welcomed and included when I feel care, and not obligation, is the motivation.

A Generation Who Feel They Don't Belong

I teach at a selective university. The students that get in here are smart. They're engaged. They've got a lot going for them. The work of the university revolves around them. And yet so many of them in this generation feel alienated and beset with imposter syndrome. They feel they don't belong. They have literally been accepted and welcomed in by the university, but at some deeper level, they don't buy it. What little nefarious whisper have they heeded to feel that this circle doesn't include them?

Some may say it's because they don't feel special anymore. They used to be among the smartest, most capable students in their high schools. Now they look left and right, and there seem to be smarter, more capable peers everywhere. Big fish, small pond syndrome.

Well, yes, but why feel like an imposter instead of thinking, "Wow, look at all these smart, talented people! How lucky I am to be among them! No doubt I will be able to learn and contribute more from my association with them. And no doubt I will be able to contribute in some way, small or large, to their betterment."

Okay, this might sound absurd to our ears, but why is that? These are rational statements. These are the ideas that we as faculty and administration continually share with the students and among ourselves about them. They only sound absurd when scarcity and competition form your generation's basic understanding of social interaction, when we are far removed from a general mindfulness of life, let alone seeking the sacred and abundant society we yearn for in our moments of inspiration.

Mindfulness, whether in an individual, a university, or a society, will respect the gifts of all, look to all with inquisitive eyes, and wait for the flowering of each one's genius.

This is utopia, right? This is also a play rehearsal.

We have a different model at our fingertips, and it is a cornerstone of our sacred space. And it can help restore a sense of belonging. Sure, there are always problems one can find, but there is so much we in the theatre get right! The decentering of competition. The palpable, pushing aside of ego. The giddy celebration when someone makes a creative breakthrough. The clocklike refinement attained through repetition. The gentle correction of a trusted collaborator in an exercise of exploration. The melting of hearts in a common and treasured enterprise. If we enter as strangers, we depart as friends.

Friends, we have a lot to share with the world that doesn't even know this much. Some of our hangups do merit attention, and they include the recrudescence of ego and competition, the perennial foe of perfectionism, and the stifling of creativity common in hierarchies.

Still, as we magnify the good, we make way for the great.

4

Tending to our Duties

If theatre is the temple of story, we are the attendants of the sacred fire. As attendants, we all have different duties. These duties may be highly specified, such as in a large, established company, or manifold and shifting in a smaller ad hoc company, or you could have anything in between. My comments may often land near the middle range, where university and local theatre companies dwell, but please extrapolate to your case.

As participants in the process—whether a play reading or a full production, it's good to be clear what our duties are from the beginning. There are universal duties: showing up on time, showing respect to others, communicating with the director or stage manager, etc... At base, the job for each one of us is to participate in the creative synthesis of rehearsal in an open-minded and attentive way and to commit to each performance in a full-hearted and disciplined manner.

Ideally, each participant's role and duties would be clear and understood by all involved. Some companies host a meet and greet at their first rehearsal, where all participants attend and have a chance to introduce themselves. This is good for creating a sense of company and sharing a vision for the larger undertaking. One may get a sense of how their duty fits in with others.

It is most important that an individual knows what their role is, what is expected of them, and what contributions they may make. Not everyone has the same expectations for certain titles and different companies have different collaborative sensibilities, and so it may be better to err on the side of caution and explicitly go through roles and expectations. If you don't know, bring it up. Most likely, the director, stage manager or producer (if one is present) will be able to either articulate the duties and expectations or consult with you on how you may best serve the process.

Example of the Actor

Acting is the most fundamental duty in our sacred space. Practically speaking, however, actors have varying intentions in taking on the characters they do. Some take on certain roles for the experience, or to work with a certain director, or because they love the play, or it's the role of a lifetime, or they need the paycheck, or maybe it's the only role they've been offered in a while. Whatever the intentions and however deep the level of interest, the duties are pretty much the same.

An example of a consciously rendered list of duties for an actor might be as follows:

- attend rehearsals, minimize and communicate time conflicts
- analyze my character with character study and breakdown of objectives

- keep clear notes of blocking and check in with SM if questions
- memorize lines by (specify dates: Scene 1..., Scene 2...)
- practice monologues, tricky areas
- ascertain time in rehearsal to work specific difficult scenes with partner
- take time for body and vocal warmup before rehearsal runs
- eat well, strive to sleep, avoid overtaxing body and inviting sickness
- invite family & friends to show

In addition to this, there are certain rules of the road the actor should recognize. They must, for example, be flexible to mold their growing understanding of their character to the company's growing understanding of the play as a whole. It is not the prerogative of an actor to commit to an approach to their character that is clashing with the director's vision or other actors' creative choices. We seek a harmonization of these things, starting traditionally with the playwright's vision—if there is a playwright.

Beyond the above-listed duties, an actor may decide they wish to take extra time to develop a connection to the character by, say, spending an afternoon walking through the city dressed and acting like the character. They may wish to write a journal in the character's voice. This is all in pursuit of a deeper bond with the character, but it does not replace or change the duty for the actor to learn their lines or blocking on time. Duty comes first.

Let's say an actor friend does not consciously consider what their duties are, but instead takes a more free or intuitive approach. But let's say they go to the first rehearsal, read though the script, and suddenly a different list of duties is burned in their mind that reads like this:

- Go to the gym
- Cut carbs, drink protein shakes
- Schedule spa appointments for tanning / hair removal / makeover

This is, of course, because there was a scene where the actor must take off their shirt, and they are feeling self-conscious about their body image. And although it doesn't seem that important a scene in the play, the actor doesn't want this to be a moment of shame in front of family, friends, and the general public. One would hope, in such a case, the actor would speak candidly with the director. And if the director also believes the scene is not so important and could just as easily be performed with a T-shirt, this might make a world of difference in the actor's experience. They may be able to concentrate then on the essentials.

Duties are not written in stone. But it's better when we are in conscious control of them. It's also better when we communicate priorities regarding our duties in a particular production.

Duty and Sacrifice

Let's agree to a distinction between our duty to a production and what we are willing to sacrifice for that production. This is an area that sometimes gets muddied, and we may benefit from clarity here. If duty is what gets a show on its feet, sacrifice is what makes it fly. That being said, the latter must be purely voluntary. No one else should dictate what I sacrifice. That is my offering at the sacred threshold.

For example, if a designer has a great idea late in the process, it is not their place to demand the shop commit to that. But if the design team and shop are fully in sync and joyfully wish to bring this new element into the production, let that be their contribution.

If the director wants to see more emotional truth from an actor in a scene, they may take time aside in rehearsal to coach that actor. But they cannot impose on the actor to do more than they are ready and willing to do. They should not demand extra time outside of rehearsal. More importantly, that actor may not be able or ready to properly channel such emotions, and if forced, there may be damage done. The actor is not the sacrificial lamb brought to the altar by some over-zealous director. This is not how our temple works. The product is not more important than the process.

Sacrifice is an act of love originating from the individual. It is not an act we decide for others. Yes, I fulfill my duty, but how much I sacrifice is up to me.

Regard for Certain Positions

Some of the offices in our trade garner more respect or are more highly sought after—the lead role, the featured singer, the star designer, the director … If you want to avoid the head trip of such roles, try to disregard the pomp or air that comes with the role and to focus on the task, the duty, the teamwork. And when others, through eagerness or ulterior motive, seek to lift you up, it is best to deflect such preference by emphasizing the work of the team, the service to common cause. Or as the great Dean Smith said, "When you make a basket, you point to the player who threw the pass."

This is not false modesty. It is wisdom. It is delusional in a collaborative art to not acknowledge the part played by others. Try putting on a play all by yourself.

Accept congratulations and gratitude with dignity. Absorb heartfelt expressions of appreciation of the work you've done. But as soon as we feel the balloons of praise start to lift our feet off the floor, we gotta let them go. The messenger of Greek theatre has run the marathon of the millenia separating its age from ours to share one urgent message: pride is folly; humility is wisdom.

And if you find yourself deep down still caught up in this Samsara of "respect for persons," this internalized partiality to position, maybe practice humility and deflection anyway. Fake it till you make it, as they say. It is essential etiquette.

All ministrations round this sacred fire are vital, they deserve respect and they should be completed with dignity. Here I want to lift up the assistant stage managers and backstage crew, who might be minimized in the celebrations of opening night. If the audience doesn't know who they are, the director should. So if you bring flowers for the actors, consider bringing them for the crew as well.

The Beatitudes of Stage Management

Blessed are the timekeepers;

Highly praised the ones who keep us on schedule.

Blessed are those who make that schedule;

They did not know how many conflicts the actors truly had.

Blessed are the patient in their roles;

Most praised are those who are able to flow with the vicissitudes of ill-health and woes of transportation.

Blessed are the flexible, for they will not snap under pressure.

Blessed are those who see things in clear perspective;

Happy are they who recognize—at the end of the day, it is just a play.

5

Proficiency and Excellence

A further word about duty—this time regarding the quality of our work, and I hope articulating it might help dispel some misunderstanding and some feelings of anxiety and impostorism. Our duty is to do the tasks we are assigned at a proficient level. If we are able to achieve excellence or inspiration or genius, that's great, but our duty is to be proficient. We do not owe anyone a level of excellence beyond our readiness to produce it.

Our work is a craft. Artistic excellence is a lifelong pursuit. Artistic proficiency, however, is attainable with some training and a certain amount of time and attention. You do have to get your hours in, but for most positions we have a fairly effective, if unofficial, apprentice system in the theatre trade. One may join a show at any level of skill and you will usually find there's a position you can fill. Smaller acting roles, assistant positions, amateur productions, these are all a great training ground. As you work, you grow.

I don't know so much about other parts of the world, but I believe the general standard of American theatre is quite high in its ability to deliver a show to an audience basically on time and as advertised. Certainly, there are horror stories / cautionary tales that may flood through the mind of an experienced theatre practitioner. Still, I would call those exceptions to the rule. Our trains do run on time, even when the behind-the-scenes of it is nail-biting. This tells me our capacity for collaboration is considerable and significant.

What about the quality of that work? Here I offer only praise and encouragement. Some might choose to frame the theatre work they encounter according to classifications such as Peter Brook's "deadly" and "immediate" designations. This certainly satisfies a critical itch we like to scratch. But when I think of theatre as a sacred space and theatre workers as striving servants to that process, my desire to evaluate it critically is changed. I want to look for the good. I want to see how they are succeeding. If they haven't discovered fire, I want to see what sparks they are making. I want to know what the big story is. All these people came together to tell me a story. As an audience member, I want to do my job and contribute my altruistic attention. I want to find the light.*

Knowing our Place in the Making of Magic

Our work is a craft, but it bumps up against the great Mystery. When that mystery is revealed in a flash of an artist's work, it has a mesmerizing effect on the viewer. If the person replicates it, we call them a genius. We soon expect the person to deliver that effect on a regular basis.

---

* I don't know exactly how to apply this to a commercial theatre that charges $200 or 300 for a seat.

An entire commercial empire on TV is dedicated to discovering such genius in the performing arts, especially among the young. These shows cycle through so many talented, hopeful individuals who have bought into the idea that this is the proper forum to channel their spiritual gifts. It seems harmless. The shows playfully acknowledge the idolatry of it. Idolatry is not harmless. You cannot capture the thrill of the Colosseum without the carnage, and here that carnage is psychological and delayed. Perhaps the most widespread negative effect is a generation that believes this is the inevitable path of talent. And we end up with millions who sing their heart's song into the void of social media, seeking likes and self-esteem and never quite grasping the function of the arts is to bring us closer to community and release us from the limitations of self.

In the theatre, our duty is not to be a genius. We don't have to take on that burden. We are enough without needing to prove ourselves or to prove that we are better. Our duty is to show up and to strive and to join in with our collaborators in the work of telling the story. Some of us may experience flashes of brilliance early on, but it's important to separate ourselves from those emanations. Zeami called this *hana,* the flower of the work. He emphasized that the early flowering is temporary and that one may find a more reliable bloom through a long-term commitment to the craft.

Let's say a young director has a victory with a show early in their career. They receive a glowing review from a theatre critic describing the brilliance of a particular scene. That young director may be inclined to repeat what they have been praised for doing. So they come to their next show with an idea of what that brilliant scene will be in this new play, and they take extra time in rehearsal—even at the expense of shaping the rest of the show. They spend hours refining it, and the actors start feeling anxious moving into tech because so much of the rest of the show feels unready. How do we imagine this show will land with audiences? Can we imagine the disappointing review waiting to be written?

That young director would probably do better to repeat the same process that yielded the desirable results in the first place. Proficient and timely execution of our task is the duty we owe to a production. Sparkle, genius, virtuosity—these are not our duty, but a gift we receive through the care and attention we pay to our duty. This is extra, and we love it, but bake the cake, then the decoration may come.

Partly, sparkle and virtuosity in our trade can be an outcome of time and attention. Or to return to the director's example: make sure the whole show is blocked and rehearsed a week before tech and that stage management and actors are given what they need, then take the extra time to sharpen those key moments. Mold the gold, then add the jewels.

The Delusions of a Young Actor

In high school, I had a blossom—at least when it came to acting. I had a natural gift when performing inside that imaginary conceit that had so dazzled me. This gift was largely uncontrolled though. Some nights the audience seemed dazzled. I was on fire! I mean, lovely Lynne Vernon fell for me after one blazing performance as Pippin. (Of course that flared out within weeks.) Other nights were dismal, at least they felt that way once I saw the lethargic reactions and heard the obligatory applause. Oh! The bipolar rhythm was being set in motion: quick short bursts of beauty and elation, followed by long spells of flaw-fixation, dwelling on mistakes and feeling a mortifying sense of letting down the crowd on these "off nights."

This, my friends, stemmed from a deep misunderstanding of our sacred space. I was deluded to think that I was responsible, that the make-or-break element was in my control. Brilliance is not summoned by force of will, and genius is not subservient to talent. The Muse is not an underling to be ordered about, but a treasured guest that will often come when invited in a spirit of hospitality.

Sacred space is where miracle moments emerge like water from a well. Our job is to tend to the mechanism and to ALLOW.

An Apology for the Seeker of Perfection

Perfectionism is a noxious species and needs to be weeded out of our garden. Not least because it stifles the work and prevents our growth. At the same time, the artist who pursues excellence may well set before themselves the very highest standard. Perfection is a noble horizon to chase.

Some pursue the refinement of their craft through productivity, regularly turning out work that grows in competence and effect as they go. The writer is up early, their drafts are submitted on time, and when the time comes, their piece is ready. Even if it is not perfect. The next project will be better. They find their audience and their audience finds them, and it is a mutually beneficial enterprise. Assuming one stays away from the sauce, this is the pathway of the successful artist.

Then there are those who pursue their craft, whether deliberately or not, with no regard for audience. They get a perfect idea and an idea for perfection in their head, and they pursue only this idea, sometimes in fits and starts, other times zealously. Others grow enthusiastic when they hear the idea and sniff the inspiration, but when the right moment to present arrives, the piece is not ready, because it is not perfect. The audience dissipates and is gone when the piece finally arrives in its splendid condition. There is no one left to witness. This is the path of the frustrated artist.

Or is it?

Thoreau tells the following story in *Walden*. I share it not as a practical model for theatre making, but as a reminder of the essentially mystical character of our work.

> *There was an artist in the city of Kouroo who was disposed to strive after perfection. One day it came into his mind to make a staff. Having considered that in an imperfect work time is an ingredient, but into a perfect work time does not enter, he said to himself, It shall be perfect in all respects, though I should do nothing else in my life.*
>
> *He proceeded instantly to the forest for wood, being resolved that it should not be made of unsuitable material; and as he searched for and rejected stick after stick, his friends gradually deserted him, for they grew old in their works and died, but he grew not older by a moment. His singleness of purpose and resolution, and his elevated piety, endowed him, without his knowledge, with perennial youth.*

As he made no compromise with Time, Time kept out of his way, and only sighed at a distance because he could not overcome him. Before he had found a stock in all respects suitable the city of Kouroo was a hoary ruin, and he sat on one of its mounds to peel the stick. Before he had given it the proper shape the dynasty of the Candahars was at an end, and with the point of the stick he wrote the name of the last of that race in the sand, and then resumed his work. By the time he had smoothed and polished the staff Kalpa was no longer the pole-star; and ere he had put on the ferule and the head adorned with precious stones, Brahma had awoke and slumbered many times.

But why do I stay to mention these things? When the finishing stroke was put to his work, it suddenly expanded before the eyes of the astonished artist into the fairest of all the creations of Brahma. He had made a new system in making a staff, a world with full and fair proportions; in which, though the old cities and dynasties had passed away, fairer and more glorious ones had taken their places. And now he saw by the heap of shavings still fresh at his feet, that, for him and his work, the former lapse of time had been an illusion, and that no more time had elapsed than is required for a single scintillation from the brain of Brahma to fall on and inflame the tinder of a mortal brain. The material was pure, and his art was pure; how could the result be other than wonderful?

People First

"Do not put the work ahead of the person."

"Do not put the work ahead of the person."

A mantra to ward off my inclination to focus on product over process, the what over the who, the gift offered over the heart that offers it.

In many theatre scenarios, we sometimes move along as if "the work" of the play justifies whatever actions we take in service of it. Since cast, crew, and production team have roles and responsibilities to the show, our interactions are not personal, they are just "the work."

Except it is personal.

That young actor, who is already intimidated among a more experienced company, is growing increasingly frustrated being asked to repeat the same scene multiple times "just until they get it right."

The assistant stage manager, who came to the show despite having a family member in the hospital, is spoken to sharply for looking at their phone during a scene change.

That designer spent all night working on those renderings finding the right color palette, adjusting the lines, choosing accessories that are actually in stock, but when their time to present comes up in rehearsal, the director cuts them short because the introductions went long and the actors are eager to dive into the script, and anyway the renderings can be hung on the wall…

Each incident of choosing product over process, the "show" over the people putting it on, is a blow to that show's foundation. The cracks multiply and begin to work in aggregate until you end up with hard feelings, division and backbiting, perhaps such a toxic environment that one component of the production starts to work against another.

If this seems like the most common scenario to you in your theatre experience, please know there are other models. The director and stage manager generally set the tone, but there are many ways to undergird and many ways to undermine. We must guard vigorously against care being overtaken by unfeeling ambition or expedience. The show is important, but the people in it are more important. Our art is vital, but it is not life and death. We can adjust. We can find a way to make it work. Flexibility is in our power, provided we uphold the standard of our sacred space.

Cases when I put Product before Person

In college, I think I was dazed a bit by the power of theatre to catapult an individual's ideas into a group consciousness. Discovering the fount of creativity that is directing was emboldening. You were not just thinking about how to affect an audience, but also how to get the performers where they needed to be emotionally. There were times when I was careless—when, for example, I would set my eyes on achieving a certain emotional truth coming from a character and prioritize that over the state of the actual person playing that character. One heard so many stories about the way "great directors" would use all manner of manipulation to capture the desired performances from their casts—this seemed like the job. Today looking back, I recoil a bit. When we push people harder than they are ready and willing to go, we can do more harm than good.

In teaching too, I have had to learn to lighten up. I teach a first-year seminar and use a basic Viola Spolin exercise about physical activity and concentration. Sometimes it takes a while for a student to make their breakthrough where they achieve full concentration in some mundane activity, and so I usually wait and keep encouraging them, while the other students watch. After the Covid lockdown, students were more resistant to presenting and expressing themselves openly. I remember one student really putting up a fight with this exercise. It surprised me, but I had to adjust my expectations.

I learned I can't insist, even if this is what we might think is a key learning in our craft. I can't insist anyone learn anything. They must simply be invited. Our art must be an invitation and not an imposition. This has been a lifelong learning for me.

A while back when I was first getting settled into full-time teaching, a now-former colleague of mine—a gifted actor—had written a screenplay and asked me to offer some feedback. This was an area where he was inexperienced, but he was finding a lot of joy in the writing. So, as I thought a colleague should, I went at it with a full court press with my dramaturgical analysis and offered him all kinds of useful approaches to revising his screenplay. I enthusiastically shared my ideas with him, and I could see him gradually withdrawing as he realized how far he might be from what I deemed to be a functional story. When I finished, I remember his one comment was how grateful my students must be for how thorough I was. And I never heard the screenplay mentioned again or anything about his writing interest.

I fear I may have snuffed out that little flame of joy of his with my enthusiastic fire hose of analysis, offered with care I should add! I was not seeking to douse his flame, but to make it greater. But I didn't understand the fundamental idea that one must keep one's focus on training the artist and not fixing the art. Train your sights on the soul before you and not the temporary emanation that soul has cast off.

What I could have done was to provide enough guidance to feed his flame and point him to the next stage of his development. I was trying to show him the journey to the finished product, and I lost him on the way.

Lest you worry about my gifted actor colleague, he did get me back. I later asked him to participate in a reading of a play of mine. He agreed, but then through the whole reading, he proceeded to yawn and show disinterest in what was an engaging role that he himself had enjoyed playing some months before. Whether this sabotage was conscious or not, I don't know, but I took my lumps, and I tried to learn from the experience.

Oh people... We are so... I won't say fragile, because our resilience is astonishing—so vulnerable though. So tender underneath that clamping shell. Tender beings fashion hard exteriors in hostile environments. And yet this tenderness is such a precious thing. Not the rough cage of ribs, but the pulsating organs within. This is where the magic is.

Sacred space is meant to be a safe zone for the sharing of the most intimate facets of our existence. Trust and trustworthiness in the handling are essential. When intimacy and tenderness are shared in unsafe areas, damage is done. We must practice this aspect of our craft mindfully and learn care. Infinite care, friends, is best used here.

On Collaboration

The miracle of humanity is not simply the wonder of the human mind, but the nearly infinite capacity when human minds are working in network and in common purpose. We are so immersed in this phenomenon, it's hard to gain perspective on it. The coffee you're sipping, the mug it's in, the book you're reading, the education that allows you to interpret it through the language that we share, which shapes thoughts that we think and are striving to sync—all are a result of the boundless web of humanity's integrated aspirations.

We oftentimes take it for granted or find the imperfections glaring and frustrating. And in our age, when the products of our unchecked aspirations threaten not simply our wellbeing but our existence, such frustrations are justified. Human civilization and human survival now await a grand divine directive like two clowns on a mound with the moon rising behind them.

Rather than wait, we need to act. Lucky for us, we in the theatre have gained a special understanding of cooperation, one that is rooted in structure, yet more flexible than the rigid rules and procedures common in governance or business. Even conventional directors will make room for actors' impulses to shape the staging of a play, rather than just insist on their own vision. And on the other end of the spectrum, some companies devise theatre pieces where the participant-creators have no title but full creative engagement. It's understandable that some businesses hire theatre people exactly for this embodied understanding we acquire, this capacity for ready and nimble interaction.

Starting with structure, moving to flow

A life in theatre is a life dedicated to learning how to collaborate. Just as in Thoreau's story of the artist from Kouroo, it will take many sleep cycles of Brahma for us to perfect this skill. Any creative project we take on will involve an attentive balancing of structure and flow and an open communication with one's creative partners.

Collaboration can get messy when we relax rules too quickly. People get touchy when they feel their creative boundaries are being transgressed: for example, actors giving other actors line-readings or a crew member swapping out an actor's costume for one they like better. There is a virtue to hoeing your own row.

Early on in the training of theatre practitioners, it is good to coach them in the traditional roles. They learn that the stage manager does not argue with the director about how to stage the show. Actors must learn to generally focus on their own character's journey and not meddle with other actors' processes. Set designers do not insist on their creative visions when it does not benefit the performance as a whole.

In early childhood, the impulses of play trigger both joy and frustration as children learn the possibilities and constraints of interaction. Stronger personalities may help set play in motion, but they can also bump and bruise other participants with their assertiveness. More timid individuals may enjoy the rush of creative group engagement and yet struggle to share the ideas bubbling up inside them. Ideally, play allows all types to moderate and coordinate their impulses through these early stages of socialization.

The sandbox of theatre brings together these and other personality types, just grown up now. When participants share, both giving and receiving, in harmonious fashion, all benefit from the richness of diverse personalities. When some individuals have not moderated and socialized their impulses, their engagement in theatre ... gives them another opportunity to do so. It may also test the cohesion of the group.

Fulfilling one's duty and respecting the boundaries of other participants is an essential starting place in theatre. Drama instructors will take a lot of time in planting these understandings in their young charges. At the same time, they would do well to envision the ultimate goal as the young people integrating this understanding so well that they may transcend it.

For example, an actor who is offstage during a scene will offer to help move a piece of furniture and not just assume it's a crew member's role. An assistant stage manager will speak separately to the costume designer to tell them how they're noticing one of the performers is having trouble getting a costume off in the scene change, and they will also share their idea for how this might be easily fixed.

It is not a great sign when the spirit of a production is "That's above my pay grade" or "Not my circus, not my monkeys."

Suppleness and flow in our collaboration is the victory we seek, and the signs are evident: smiles, laughter, and people showing care for one another. The production is elevated in such an environment, especially because people are joyfully bringing forth their best effort.

Threats to our collaboration

So one pitfall in our work is the potential stifling of enthusiasm and creativity that a too rigid enforcement of the rules can bring. Perpetuators of this may include insecure (or simply old-fashioned) directors. It can also be embedded in artistic institutions, where the formalities of the business side may seep into the artistic side. How fortunate those theatres that rise above this!

Another potential difficulty is the unpleasant disruption that can arise when certain personalities overextend their position into disrespect. I was once present at a tech rehearsal where a respected director was onstage and making a request of the team in the booth, and a 1st year undergraduate lightboard operator rudely shouted out the window at the director: "Hold on, Adam!"

The whole theatre went silent and all eyes widened, including the director's. He paused, and then calmly walked out the side door and back to the booth. The whole theatre remained quiet as we all looked around at each other. And then we heard the director admonishing the student from the booth: "You will not speak to me this way!" He added some other forceful, but in no way abusive, language. There was then another silence. The director walked back in the side door onto the stage and rehearsal resumed.

I tend to give a lot of slack to students, so I think about the lines of respect that we delineate. Now, was this director's response the optimal one? Perhaps, perhaps not. It certainly reinforced the hierarchy of roles. I will say what he did was far preferable than just allowing that student to show such rudeness—not just to the director, but to the collective process—without any response. The fact that he said it loud enough for us in the theatre to hear may have been part of what he wanted to achieve. I didn't take it as a warning, but rather that he was standing up for the general respectful environment he wished to foster.

I guess if I could have rewritten his line for him, I would have him say, "You will not speak to anyone that way in this rehearsal process."

In our ideal theatre, a director is not an authority to be most respected, but the point person who helps coordinate all the different creative inputs. We respect everyone and everyone's task, but we also acknowledge the director's role in making choices that benefit and unify the whole. This is the prerogative of leadership. Is it possible to have theatre without leadership? Perhaps yes. There are troupes that have a remarkably egalitarian approach. This is a high level of working, which most of the theatre world would struggle to replicate. That can be our aim, and we have the traditional roles we can lean on as needed. Let us just make sure we take on the tradition without the presumptions of superiority and hierarchy that may accompany such models.

Disrespect, insecurity, competition, cliques, backbiting—these and many other threats to the spirit of our sacred task exist, and we will never completely purge them from our midst. Every situation in art and in life will have its blend of promise and difficulty, and our growth would be stunted if this were not the case. The key is in how we respond. Do we retreat and not address it? Do we reassert authority and insist on compliance? Do we throw a tantrum and hope this show of emotional instability helps in some way? Would it be more helpful to speak with individuals about the behaviors? Or maybe we should address the whole group and begin a conversation that frames the issue as a learning opportunity?

There is no handbook for life. The book we write is our being. We sit with the questions life brings, and we listen for an answer that arises not from our anger or anxiety, but from deeper down. We bring this forward then into the plane of action, as if it were a hypothesis to a scientific question. We try it, and we see what we learn. Our collected experiences begin to better inform our responses as we go; openness brings knowledge brings wisdom. And then you find yourself trying to write it all down in a book, and in your book you write: There is no handbook for life. The book we write is our being.

Finally, I would mention that gravest, most pernicious threat to our art and to our nation. Racism is in the air we breathe, and we must vigilantly strive to clear that air in our midst. I hope recent efforts in decolonizing theatre spaces have been proving effective. The open letter "We See You, White American Theatre" in June 2020 was especially compelling, but that effort has been going on a longer time in many places. And it needs to continue. Confrontation and forbearance, heart-sharing and walking-the-line, all modes of engagement must be considered as the institutional and systemic biases and injustices are sifted. Ultimately, our goal is the same suppleness and flow in collaboration I spoke of earlier and with all people feeling welcome, feeling they belong, striving together and merging their best efforts.

How blessed those theatre makers who rejoice in our common humanity and who lovingly make space in their circle for the children of the world!

Part Two

Purpose

An Urgent Purpose

Awake to awareness, the world is but a dream
Awake to awareness, the world is but a dream
Is this what is real?

So begins Zeami's play, *Atsumori.** This Noh drama is steeped in Buddhist belief, so we recognize the lesson about the illusory material world. And yet, these verses are being said in a theatre. We generally think that the life we live is real and that theatre is a conceit of fantasy—a dream, so to speak. But here, from the stage, the play proclaims the world—the part we think is real—is a dream and then asks, is this—the experience of the play—what is real?

Does this tie back to the revelation that hit me in the 7th grade? There was a greater truth present, or at least available, in the room, and Truth is real even if the world is not. Is it possible that the stage is a gateway of the real and true? If the world is illusory, then is this illusion factory within it (i.e., the

---

* Translation by Karen Brazell

theatre) able to break through the matrix code or at least glimpse beyond it?

One may find similar sentiments and questions raised in other classical plays such as *Midsummer Night's Dream* and *Life is a Dream*.

To say the world is illusory is not to retreat from care or concern. Suffering is a call to compassion and fruitful action. To say theatre is a gateway of the real and true is not to prioritize it over the world. We live in the world; to try to live in art is delusional. That theatre is both dreamlike and a doorway to the real is a paradox, and a worthy one to ponder.

A Communal Dream

Dreams offer a striking parallel to drama. When we go to sleep, we shut the door on the world outside, settle into bed, close our eyes, slip into the darkness, and awake into a new world, where new circumstances confront us, and we compliantly engage as if, yes, we were on a road trip to Florida with a coworker from 10 years ago, and yes, the geese are walking along the side of the road, and yes, suddenly the bridge we are on is going straight down and the cars and the geese are now moving into free fall, and why aren't the geese flying, and we fall but we never hit bottom.

In the theatre, we manufacture a purposefully rendered communal dream. We sequester ourselves, shut the doors to the outside life, put away its concerns for the time being, *silence and put our phones away*, then a hush spreads over us like a spell, darkness descends like a shared submission to sleep, and even as in a dream, a new world appears before us, so very different than our waking world. Soon, we find ourselves immersed in lives different from our own, and yet we start to relate, then we begin rooting for some individuals, getting angry with others, then getting angry with those we rooted for earlier, until we find ourselves weeping because someone steps on a glass figurine.

"Why cry?" your stem-major roommate with a frozen heart asks when you get back home and try to explain the experience. "It's not your glass figurine."

"It's not about the figurine. It's about what it represents!"

"What's it to you? These people aren't even strangers, they don't exist."

Clearly your roommate is upset about your leaving unwashed pots in the sink two nights in a row.

"So you are treating these non-existent strangers with more care and consideration than you showed at your last family gathering when you complained about relatives not bringing enough food."

Your roommate with the frozen heart, who has obviously been talking to your mother, is not wrong, but neither are they right.

Through the story and the fiction, through the obviously artificial conceit, a light shines. It is the true and the real that finds us in the midst of this masquerade, but we never quite know what mask it will be wearing. That is, from night to night, different aspects, different lines, different character dynamics will impact us.

Dreams come to us each night, tailored to the moment we are in by some super-rational self or collective unconscious.

They come with purpose. They come with no other goal but our betterment.

Of course, there are different species of dream. Some are clearly a flushing out of the neural pipelines, while others signal some meaning through the dusky mist to be pondered and divined for their subtle, idiosyncratic symbolism. Still others are as a cataract plunging on the chest, or an arrow shot through the apple atop one's head. Some dreams scare us so much we wake up gasping and grasping, so grateful for the clemency of the quiet night. Others share a vision or euphoria, a reunion with a lost loved one from which we never wish to return.

But return we do. Are we changed?

Dreams have messages, and attentiveness to them aids in the carrying out of an examined life. Their message and their purpose, however, are not always easily discernible or rational or moralizing. Sometimes there is just something in the fully engaged, yet disembodied experiencing of them that makes a needed adjustment to our being.

This is a noble model to reflect on as we ponder what content we place in our sacred space. Purpose without puritanism, message without manipulation. Limitless possibilities.

Articulating Purpose

In some of my classes, I begin the semester by asking the students to articulate the purpose of drama. Some of them are brand new to theatre, some know quite a good deal about it. The answers run the gamut of possibilities of artistic intention.

They range from the straightforward ("to entertain") to the Classical ("to edify") to the Romantic ("to express oneself") to the Realist ("to diagnose social ills") to the Avant-garde ("to provoke") and beyond. I don't remember ever hearing a "wrong" answer, and I fill the blackboard with the myriad answers.* It's an important learning for us from the very beginning of our study of drama not to limit the possibilities of our art.

To say theatre's purpose may be expressed in a host of ways is not to say there is no urgent or central purpose. The students' points of view spread out in complement like the points of a circle surrounding a center that evades words.

Oskar Eustis spoke to the question of central purpose in a 2018 Ted Talk connecting theatre and democracy. He highlighted how theatre builds our sense of empathy and our sense of community. He also emphasized theatre's use of dialogue, and how dialogue is effective at eliciting the truth. Eustis says, *"The truth can only emerge in the conflict of different points of view. It's not the possession of any one person."*

Empathy. Community. Dialogue. This is at the core of our purpose. Theatre, like all the arts, is here to serve us—as in humanity, audience and artists. The question then becomes how do we best use this tool, this sacred venue, to serve our current situation?

Great! One of theatre's principal virtues is its spontaneity, its liveness, its alterability up through the very moment of execution. This finds it in company with the other performing

* Yes, we still have some blackboards at UNC.

arts of dance and music. The separation of these three is a cultural peculiarity of the west, and while theatre does have a value and a potency in its refined form, refinement has its drawbacks. Rice, flour, sugar, medicinal foods—all are generally absorbed better by the human mechanism in their holistic form.

Let us consider theatre as medicine. This goes for music and dance, as well. Here I speak of medicine in its broadest sense—that which brings balance and restores to wholeness. We learn this idea from Native American thinking and that of other indigenous and non-western societies. Of course, we should approach this task with humility and a sense of service to community rather than a patronizing sense of "knowing better." We are not seeking to fix others, but to heal and comfort, to contribute a gift to the common welfare.

Let's say we were looking after the health of a friend who has been going through some difficulty. There is no single approach we can take to help our friend. Different days will dictate the different ways. On Monday, they're sad, so we tell a story to cheer them up. On Tuesday, they're edgy and talkative, so we listen and help them process. On Wednesday, they're restless and tired of words, so we go on a long walk together. One day it's laughter, the next day it's tears, and then comes a day filled with both.

As makers of theatre, let us look at the world around us. Let's say I see a bunch of sad, isolated faces in the street. What if I concocted a five-minute piece of guerilla theatre to bring joy and a little community to strangers on the streets. If you're angry at the complacency you see in the people around you, channel that fire by directing a play to awaken alertness and compassion.

Suit the action to the need; judge the need with care. We may not know how to address some general societal conflagration, but we can be attentive to the signs that are showing in our lives and those around us. This way we extend out our care not as if for strangers and fictions, but as if for family and friends. Empathy, community, dialogue.

There is no single solution to the question of approach. Consider: Artaud's burning victim signaling through the flames and Brecht's Alienation Effect—two urgent yet diametrically opposing theatrical concepts—both emerged in 1930s Europe. Both were responding to a deep, receding cultural ebb—the tsunami drawback that preceded the tidal wave of world war.

Our world is sick. Our friends, family, and everyone else is in deep need—ourselves included. The urgency has never been greater.[†] This is no cause to be frantic. Frantic energy lends itself to scarcity thinking, which yields greater harm than good. It is time to return to mindfulness, to focus on our task.

On the altar of the stage, we strive together to kindle a sacred fire, a story of intentional design. We tend and we watch, with the audience, as the delightful conceit ignites, swells, peaks and crumbles, even as wood moves to ash. The heat is our enthusiasm, joy and empathy, and the light of meaning shines out, at once universal and touching each one differently.

† At the time I'm writing this, the Doomsday clock set by the Bulletin of Atomic Scientists is 85 seconds to midnight, the closest we've ever been to global catastrophe.

9

The Message I'm Hearing

Our purpose as artists will translate into our work as message. In tending to our sacred space, we must take care with message and be aware of what we're putting out there. Here I'm separating message from story and genre. We do well to welcome a wide array of stories, genres, and all manner of points of view. Message is the meaning we leave with, and meaning is the soul's food. A play is a philosophy on its feet.

Now there are messages that dim our light and others that desecrate our space. That latter category includes racist and ultranationalist propaganda and work that abuses or demeans individuals or groups. I won't waste time speaking further of such an obvious position.

Satire of public figures is an interesting category here. It is a foundation stone of our artform and a bellwether for free speech. It can also do harm. With *The Clouds,* Aristophanes helped turn the public against Socrates, and that great light of wisdom was snuffed out as Greek democracy corroded.

One key success of our theatre in the past several decades has been the attention paid to representation of formerly excluded or marginalized voices. We now see, for example, many more plays written by and featuring people of color in the mainstream American theatre. This is a big win for us. Such representation is a vital step in restoring the sanctity of our stage. We hope that such expansion also brings a broadening of message.

Sometimes, there is a risk of homogenization happening at the level of message, even when we have greater inclusion with, say, cultural or gender identity. There can be a party line we subtly reinforce that is the opposite of our intention in welcoming in more voices. The idea is not to just have more people of various backgrounds and life experiences reassert the status quo. This is not the revolution we seek. What we want is these people to bring their unique perspectives to the table. Let all bring their special dish to this big potluck. It shouldn't all be potato salad, no matter the seasoning.

The Gospel of the Unbounded Heart

I have a pet theory that the American theatre loosely subscribes to a de facto religion, or a belief system, anyway, and I have somewhat glibly labeled it the "Gospel of the Unbounded Heart." It conforms pretty well to Romantic individualism, and I think it goes back in our playwriting maybe to Eugene O'Neill and lingers up to this day. By no means all, but so many American plays sit comfortably in the pews of this chapel. If one were to translate the metaphysical subtext of these plays, it might sound like this:

"Do that which is in your heart. Your heart knows best—better than your government, better than your church, better than your

parents. Do not give in and conform to the rules of institutions that claim they know more than you. This independence may lead to difficulty and even death, but you will be on the side of the right if you follow your heart. And the angels will weep for you—and by the angels we mean the audience, because we really don't subscribe to the Christians' worldview. They, after all, wanted us to subdue our hearts with the rules of their institutions."

This is my playful attempt at summing up a consistent message I've been hearing over my years of attending plays. It is a distinct perspective from the famous European models emerging about the same time. Brecht had little respect for institutions, but he was also highly suspicious of individual ambitions. Absurdism found little dignity in any sort of stand the individual might take. This gospel is partially an outgrowth of American optimism.

Now personally I have a set of beliefs at some variance with this. Many of us who work in the theatre do. It could be that this figurative playing area was worked out as a pluralistic compromise among the diverse beliefs that show up to watch and to make theatre.*

Many of my favorite plays proclaim this worldview, and I often find I'm very much behind such a message. If I'm watching *The Crucible*, I'm not thinking to myself: "Come on, John and Elizabeth! Obviously, the judges have your best interest in mind. Just go along with them and everything will work out fine."

* I will not attempt to contextualize this bent in American theatre with patterns in the greater society, as that is beyond my capacity and the scope of this book.

In other cases, I find it quite limiting—almost as if this were a litmus test to check that a play has the right pH for acceptance by the status quo. At one of the last plays I attended, I had the thought of this chapter drifting in my mind, and then the gentle protagonist came out and said, "I don't believe in God, and I don't believe in heaven and hell." And it seemed almost as if it were meant to disarm us: you don't have to worry about me; I fit in this world here. The matter of the character's belief or disbelief was not relevant to the development of the story, and it was addressed no further. I had to ask myself: would it be so easy for a central character on the professional stage to come out and say, "I believe in God, I attend church, and I'm happy," and then for the matter to be dropped?

In that scenario, I feel like the audience—trained in the mores of this institution we attend—would expect that statement to be tested as the story unfolds. A gun introduced must be fired, apparently. And the gun in this case is a character assumed to be imbalanced because their choices are restricted or bound by an authority other than their own desire.

I cannot dispute the viability of plays that champion human rights and freedoms. I have written such plays. I simply suggest that we make sure we welcome in complementary messages. A body grows weak eating only one food; the soul too needs a diverse and well-balanced diet. The unrestrained individualism in the United States is at toxic levels. I have friends and students here from other countries that break down crying at how disconnected they feel from other people since they have been in this country. We should pay attention to the degree to which our theatre is, perhaps unwittingly, reinforcing this imbalance.

Alternative Messages in the Mix

A welcome expansion from this sort of messaging are the stories we have with a more communal philosophy pervading them. This is a characteristic of many plays upwelling from the African diaspora. Some famous 20th Century examples might be the movement from "I" to "we" that we get in *For Colored Girls* and the forging of the Younger family into a collective protagonist in *A Raisin in the Sun.* In *Fences,* divine salvation is not individual but collective, because the growth and progress of the new generation act as a saving grace to the older, seemingly broken ones.

It is not only through the presentation of diverse faces and bodies on our stages that our theatre will be saved. It will also require allowing the stories emerging from the deep wells of world culture and spiritual traditions. It will take the contemporization of those traditions by individuals still connected to them, and not just disenchanted voices displaying cultural questioning and deconstruction of tradition for otherwise indifferent audiences. A deconstructive mindset can be habit-forming, and at a certain point, one is left only with rubble. We grow by starting not with what is perfect but what is good, and with our attention, we make it better.

Classic plays often assert themes that challenge the inherent hegemony of the individual. Some might share a Christian providential lesson, where divine wisdom and mercy free the soul from clinging to its misguided views and desires. *A Christmas Carol* is the unshakable model.

Other classic plays emphasize or interrogate the duty the individual has to the state and cosmos. *Antigone* and *Julius Caesar* are still performed frequently. In modern productions of Sophocles or Shakespeare, however, do we emphasize the psychology over the cosmology? Perhaps we feel such themes have aged better? How comfortable are we in considering that our lives are not quite our own? My students often vigorously reject the workings of Fate in their lives. And yet can one imagine a generation more anxious of its looming future, or more incapacitated by the manipulating systems of the status quo, and thus more consigned to its fate?

An Encroaching Nihilism

I detect a sense of purposelessness in our midst in recent years. Many of the plays I'm seeing seem to be searching for purpose, as if the artists are struggling with vision. The old answers don't seem to be satisfying any more in an age when down is up and up is down.

I saw a celebrated contemporary play last night, as it happens, that I found enchanting in its gentle, yet hyper-realistically slow descent into meaning. After having dedicated almost 3 hours to that journey, I then learned the message: people are selfish. What?! Talk about an unsatisfying end to a delightful yarn! So did I stand up and protest? Of course not. I know the actors, I know the director. I knew half the people in the room and most of the people backstage. I stood up and applauded and did so happily because they had done a great job. The acting was marvelous, and I had lost myself in the world and in the characters. But there at the end, I was jolted by this message of despair. I had grown to see these characters, imperfect as they were, as seekers of connection and improving as they go. Yet I felt the playwright had given up on them and deliberately snared them in a plot device to expose the characters'—and by extension, humanity's—essential corruption.

I full-heartedly believe a playwright should be free to write their story the way they will, and yet I also felt betrayed by being led along a path, assured by the trappings of truth, only to find a deposit of what I take to be fool's gold. Perhaps another way to express it is I felt this sacred space had been—in some regard—diminished or darkened.

Now, is despair in humanity a desecration and therefore not allowable on our stage? I don't think we need to approach it that way. The stage can survive, but we probably benefit more by putting the issue up for dialectical questioning. This is the power of dialogue to reveal broader truths. So we ask the question of the stage: are people essentially selfish? Then we watch as the stage does its magic and reveals, through differing character perspectives, the various positions we think of and ones we hadn't thought of before. Everyone may take away something a little different, but such is the nature of our sacred fire's light.

We will circle back to this question of purpose, but first let's consider the historical perspective.

10

Our Place in History

All things are in process, rising and returning
Plants blossom for a season, then return to the root.[*]

When we look over the centuries at the history of theatre we see there are discernible cycles, patterns that indicate an organic process at work. Just like the seasons, we have a period of dormancy, of flowering, of fruition, and of decay. If you look, say, at a fruit tree, there's that wonderful and fairly narrow stretch in the cycle when you can enjoy the fruit right off the tree. So too, there seem to be, in theatre history, short bursts of true creative thriving—when creators and audience and patrons are locked in sync supporting a system at its creative peak.

The great names of classical theatre—such as Sophocles, Zeami, Shakespeare—sit atop such peaks. Yes, they were geniuses, but they were also the beneficiaries of their moment in history, bright stars in a larger constellation. Often, there

---

* Lao Tzu, Tao Te Ching. #16. Translation by Sam Torode.

was no more than a generation or two of ideal creative equilibrium, and this ephemerality seems determined by larger cultural forces outside the control of creative people tending to their craft.

Such is the temporary quality of all organic life. If one may enjoy fruit or theatre outside of its peak season, this is owing to the science of preservation—whether a recipe for cherry jam or the institutionalization of a dramatic genre supported by government subsidy and a steady flow of aficionados and tourists.

Once we get to modern drama, the picture gets murkier than in pre-modern contexts. This is not because we somehow stand outside cultural forces or the ebb and flow of historical patterns, but rather because we sit too closely to see objectively the full scope of where we are relative to the whole. In trying to discern our own place in history, it may help to look a little closer at the phases of fruition that pre-modern drama passed through.

Early on in the cycle, the stories tend to be more idealistic, perhaps naïve, underdeveloped; they may be somewhat incoherently structured, but urgent and hopeful in the effect sought. This is tart fruit, and this phase can last a considerable time. This is the era of Sarugaku and Thespis at the City Dionysia. The best-preserved example we have of this phase is the centuries of mystery plays that sprung up in Europe's Middle Ages.

As the cycle nears its peak, the work finds a better balance, more structure, perhaps a more realistic expectation. This is the sweet stage. The scripts from these days come down to us as if they were special seeds carefully preserved for posterity. These are the works that fill our anthologies.

Late stage work we might describe as bitter fruit: antihero stories; a more cynical, often materialistic outlook; emphasis on spectacle and taboo-busting; amoral or even immoral messaging. There is a lack of concern with earlier aesthetics. Nihilism shows up partly as a bucking of early structure. This work generally doesn't hold long. Audiences recede, and government institutions withdraw support or they topple. Among the more striking examples of this phase is the decadence and perversity that overtook Kabuki as it sought to gratify its redlight district crowds in the 19th Century.

Materialism, emphasis on spectacle, taboo-busting, anti-hero stories, nihilism—these might sound very familiar as we survey the contemporary entertainment industry in the U.S. I am not sure, however, that we can simply conclude we are in a universal artistic downturn and therefore might as well go looking for a calling in healthcare. Theatre may yet have a purpose for us.

A Theatre of the World

The modern world represents a paradigm shift from historical precedent in several ways. For one thing, we do not face in the modern world the sorts of desolate dormant periods that waylaid pre-modern drama, periods which might last for centuries and were the result of falling empire, invasions, and the breakdown of order. Art is not possible when citizens are fighting for their lives or struggling to feed their families. Yes, creative capacity is always present in people, but only the sanctuary of civilization can nurture the collective endeavor of

Art. Creativity is a perennial; Art is a cultivar. And we see modern civilization marches on despite social disruptions, war, and economic turmoil. If one region declines, another rises, and the work continues.

Modern drama, just like modern civilization, is not fixed in one land or culture. It may have begun in northern Europe in the 19th Century, but it has long ago left such confines. Creative influences now fly around the globe at light speed, while influential creatives fly from continent to continent in less than a day. A Chinese playwright friend of mine recently sent me feedback on my play (about a Russian writer) after returning home to the Netherlands from the premiere of her work in Shanghai. Her next piece will be in South Korea. Another friend who lives part time in South Africa asked me to send some of my short plays to workshop with folks in Zambia. Professionals and amateurs, we have access to the greatest unifying and equalizing resource humanity has ever produced: the beautifully named World Wide Web.

Modern drama built on the foundations of that which preceded it, and not just the European models. In their frenzied ambition to save or scold humanity, theatre makers explored and expanded, exploited and exploded. A century or two of avant-garde ambition has yielded a wide array of performance styles and production approaches, from the widespread success of lifelike acting techniques to the bizarre and incomprehensible staging of Dada, to the influential, though still estranging world of Absurdism; from a highly ritualized ceremony in a forest to an immersive, semi-spontaneous happening on a city street; from the voyeurism of peeking into an apartment as a couple grumbles and eats steak to the fantastic lift of having savannah wildlife walk by you, operated by human puppeteers, in a 3000 seat touring house.

Nearly all imaginable versions, inversions, and subversions of dramatic form—stretching story, character, theme, and event; engaging all manner of movement, gesture, language, whether predetermined or improvised; merging with other artforms, upsetting norms of actor-audience boundaries, claiming the world as stage—all these have been attempted. The era of formal innovation seems to be nearing its conclusion. Congratulations, theatre folk! We've mapped Planet Theatron.†

Now that we basically know we can do most anything, we may focus our attention on what we may do most effectively. And we arrive back at the question of purpose.

Partly, theatre folks may be feeling a sense of purposelessness because the promise of finding new forms is vanishing. Some of us had operated with the quixotic assumption that if we just found the right form, our theatre would prove effective and we and the audience would be delivered and the world renewed.

And we were right. That has occurred. Thousands of times, probably millions of times. Living in the Day of Judgment, you come to realize that in each and every moment a sacred victory is possible. There is no finality to our work here. Awake to awareness: our work is ourselves.

---

† Such a claim is always wrought with peril. It's true the digital world may open a new plane of innovation, but whether that qualifies as theatre is a question to be discussed.

You may have noticed that I pivoted away from discussing the future of American theatre and instead focused on the larger picture of modern drama meaning world drama. I guess I believe any analysis of the United States of America considered in isolation from the rest of the world is backward-looking and unfruitful.

I am a citizen of the world. I make theatre locally because I care about the people of the world, and I want to do my humble part to help that world.

As I write these words, the Artemis II astronauts are making their way to the moon. They will encounter magnificent and challenging experiences, and they will also find the same lifeless rock as their predecessors left behind fifty years ago, the rock that makes them look back in awe at the precious blue pearl on the horizon. Astronauts are like those who have near death experiences; most of them come back with a sensation they can't quite put into words. It's just the exquisite beauty and the harmonic singleness of the earth. There are no flaws, there are no boundaries.

They are now sending us back pictures.

Our sacred circle.

This sacred space.

11

Finding Our Wellspring

The young come to purpose with the fiery engine of ambition. Learning the art is a natural starting place for a young artist's purpose. Honing one's craft, studying its history, learning the ins and outs of the trade, these should be a student's and an apprentice's focus. Young theatre artists should generally say yes to the opportunity that comes to them, even if it's outside the specialty they're considering. Proficiency is gained through breadth of experience.

Once we begin to gain proficiency, ambition may start to want something more. Our purpose will start to move away from a consuming focus on craft, and we will do well to start thinking about purpose. Why do I do this work? What kind of plays or other productions do I wish to take part in? Do I simply accept any work? Do I begin to choose projects based on the quality of the show or even the message of the show?

Let's say an actor has an audition spree, trying out for a dozen roles, and let's say they get cast in several different plays. Should the actor, by default, choose a) the largest role,

b) the largest paycheck, or c) the opportunity that presents the best networking possibility? That's how the choice might appear to them. Notice, however, each of these choices implies a purpose indistinguishable from career ambition.

What if that actor chooses a project because of the play's quality? Let's say they have two options: One play is very popular and features dynamic roles and good writing, but the feeling it leaves the audience with is deeply pessimistic. Another play provides less of an acting challenge, but the play as a whole is powerful and leaves the audience with a feeling of hope. Which one will the actor choose? If the actor's purpose is oriented more to creative excellence, they might choose the former. A purpose centered on community impact would lean to the latter.

Similar choices around ambition and purpose apply no doubt to directors, designers, and others. Theatre crew are part of the storytelling team as well, and they care about the impact of the work they are involved with too. Often, they know the actors' lines just as well as the actors. For all concerned, it is better to align our choices with a consciousness of purpose.

Finding Company, Building Community

The proper role of ambition is to lift us to a place where we may perform optimally. With theatre these days, finding and holding such a stable spot is tricky. Unless you make a home in one of the few resident companies out there, a professional designer, actor, or director has be a freelancer and bounce around a city or a country acquiring gigs through hustle and sweat. Perhaps good word-of-mouth begins to smooth the path at a certain point. Academia is a haven for many of us, provided that teaching and mentoring is also fulfilling to the artist and their purpose.

Ideally, theatre artists fall into company with collaborators they like and mesh with well, and they make time to make good art together. This might be in a professional, community or academic theatre settings. Teaching drama at a high school is an all-in gig, but if you choose to see the students as your collaborators, you can make good art together.

Good art is not perfect art. Good art is the proper activation of our sacred space!

If one finds such a setting, a community or network of compatible artists, ambition should probably be taken down a notch or redirected. Ambition tends to have a wandering eye. We can take that drive, which has always been looking outwardly for satisfaction or improvement, and retrain it. One obvious direction is to hone the craft further, pursuing excellence within the agreeable bounds we now find ourselves.

This comes back to purpose. If we do not consciously consider our purpose with our work, we may default to ambition for an ever-higher ascendancy in some perceived career hierarchy. True, a network of artists is not a marriage, and you may move on if you wish and without appearing before a judge. Are we acting in good faith, however, with our current collaborators when we are always seeking a "more ideal" situation?

Part of the success of consistent collaboration is the foundation of trust and understanding that is built over time working with people. Yes, we have to learn to deal with the whole person, strengths and shortcomings. Helping to build a community of trust—whether in the arts or not—is longer term work. It's like planting fruit trees. You might have to wait a while for the harvest. So many of us benefit greatly from the labors of those who came before us; we owe much to the effort and care that went into community and institution building. A theatre company, a university, a city ... the circle keeps expanding.

Divining our Purpose

As long as there is blood in our veins, the excitement of a new thing, a new venture will always grab our attention. Some of them are the train we're meant to jump on, and they'll take us where we need to go. Most we should let pass and understand that whistle to be a distraction.

There is no lasting thrill in this life. There is no way to hold and maintain the ecstatic experience of our entry into art, nor love. What lasts through the cycles of time is purpose. Purpose is the long game of art and love. Commitment is its necessary companion.

Traditionally, purpose is found in religion, but this is not so much the case these days. Theatre folk and other artists have largely taken leave of religion, at least in its organized forms. It's interesting, because I feel like, among our contemporaries, theatre folk stand out for a striking spirituality. Perhaps this relates to the empathy and understanding so central to our art.

Purpose cannot be faked ... for very long anyway. It is the wellspring of our work. If our well is dry, it will show up in our work. We may feel burnout. We may lose patience quickly with our collaborators or audience. Our thoughts and our imagination will start to shrink. If the well is dry, we will need to drill deeper down.

Art is not enough. Theatre is not enough. To use the analogy I've been using throughout the book: serving at the threshold of our sacred space is not enough. I advise every theatre artist to have a mindfulness practice, of whatever variety. First for our lives, second for our art.

We are people before we are artists. We need to approach life deliberately. If we do not, why are we messing around with the arts? Why are we risking poverty and rejection and putting our family's wellbeing at stake? Certainly, those who are only involved to express themselves or to shame their parents for neglect will be weeded out before they get to this point of reflection.

If you believe you are engaged in a sacred task, then what do you believe is sacred? Find that. And serve that. And let that be the foundation of your purpose.

And all of us must believe in at least one thing.

We must believe in people.

12

Nature and Character

People disappoint. They do. They do lousy things sometimes. Maybe they aren't thinking, but other times they just don't show up for you when you're relying on them. Or they only show up when it aligns with their self-interest. I'm not even speaking of the aggressive and harmful personalities out there. The world can be a dark place.

Now let me reframe: WE disappoint. WE do lousy things. We don't think, and we don't show up for others, or we only show up when it works for us... It's important that we don't separate ourselves from humanity when we are offering a critique of it.

How then do we have hope in the face of human failure? How do we believe in people when even our theatre is telling us people are just selfish? How do we find light to see though this darkness?

Faith.

It's a candle in the dark. And as far as I can see, it's the only antidote to despair. Hopes get crushed, but faith is a commitment to keep hoping.

Now what you have faith in is your call. Maybe it is in God or a higher power, or maybe it's in science or the working of the Universe, or maybe the source of your faith is the goodness of animals. Whatever it is, feed the flame. Voice gratitude, repeat affirmations of positivity, go to a religious service, retreat to the wilderness, or best of all, go and do service, where we commit an act of kindness for someone else—perhaps someone worse off than we are—and with no expectation of receiving anything in return. Then we try it again.

We must be the light if we find ourselves in darkness. We must be the change if we long to see the world get better. Maybe, just maybe, the key to unlocking our own faith in people can be found in witnessing our own ability to change for the better. That is another way of saying our faith in others depends on our faith in ourselves.

Human Nature vs. Human Character

If human nature is a constant, human character is the variable. That is, if people are selfish, they can also become saintly.

If a character in a play is struggling with self-centeredness, we watch in anticipation of them growing into a better version of themself. It's the same as we would watch with delight as a child learns to play more gently with others on the playground.

If human nature is a perennial, human character is the cultivar—to return to an image used earlier. We aren't perfect, but we are perfectible.* We aren't always good, but we can get better. Self-interest can move to virtuous self-interest can move to altruism can move to self-sacrifice, just as red bleeds to maroon bleeds to purple bleeds to violet.

Why am I writing these words right now? Does it basically come down to self-interest or sacrifice? Is it rooted in love for others or a desire to exalt the self? Am I looking for connection or a legacy or to cover up a sense of inadequacy? At the moment, what I'm mostly aware of is the desire to articulate this idea clearly. But I accept, on principle, that human beings are perpetually acting on a spectrum of intentions, which bleed together, much like colors on the color chart. This is our nature.

One of the mysteries of being human, however, is that we are able to focus, in moments of conscientiousness, on a desired noble motivation, as opposed to an unconscious reactive one. And in doing so, something in us grows stronger. We call this something character. This capacity to grow in character is the cornerstone of story.

A great insight in Joseph Campbell's concept of the *monomyth* is how story, myth, and dream reflect the manner of life in educating, edifying, and testing the human soul. Even if you have a hard time framing the soul in non-physical terms, this implicit function of perfectibility begs to be reckoned with.* Otherwise, what is the value of theatre? Wouldn't our efforts be worthless if theatre cannot influence human betterment?

---

* Perfection is not a destination any of us need worry about attaining, but the notion of perfectibility gives us a horizon we can ever pursue (c.f., Chapter 5).

If we go back to *Oedipus Rex,* we see that Oedipus has a wide range of motivation at the play's beginning: to save Thebes, to uphold his dignity, to assert his dominance, to protect against usurpation, to uncover the truth, to vaunt himself above the control of the gods. By the play's climax, his motivations are reduced to one: to uncover the truth.

The startling scope of activated objectives in mercurial Hamlet remains basically undiminished throughout the play, and only late in Act V, in his very last moments as he realizes his time is up, does he choose the one: to kill the evil king. This is the intention that he, in heroic posture, vowed to singularly pursue in Act I. All those competing objectives until then render Hamlet unable to act.

A story is ultimately heroic if the protagonist chooses the single, good path, even if it exposes them to harm. It is the choosing in the end of the right and the good.

Acting on a Tightrope

In this respect, I'd like to suggest an adjustment to the way we teach play analysis and acting. The great insight of 20th Century acting technique is that the actor should orient their performance not around emotion but objectives. Playing the need creates coherence and flexibility, and it mirrors more closely our approach to action in real life. My suggestion is that when we analyze a character's objectives, we narrow them down not to one superobjective, but to two.

Both of these superobjectives will spring from the character's response to the play's crisis. They should represent opposing reactions, one of which is generally conscious, and one of which is often unconscious. The actor, of course, should be aware of both.

Choose the two such that they actively lead to contradiction, which will show up as internal conflict. One represents the desire of the higher self; the other is a baser, reactive intention. Generally, the higher self manifests in the conscious mind, but this is not always the case. When articulating them, both should be put in the active "to do" form.

To stay with the Classical examples already introduced, one actor might determine that Oedipus's overarching desires are "to search out the truth" and "to crush any threat to my security." The first is certainly the consciously articulated one, while the second is revealed through his over-the-top reactions when he finds out truths he perceives as a threat to his security.

As for the infamously hesitant Hamlet, one superobjective should lead to bold action while the other should stop action in its tracks. An actor might combine "to vindicate my father" with "to avoid difficulty and engagement with the world and its pain." In this case, the first is Hamlet's conscious stated goal, while the second may come from cowardice that has grown in someone who has dedicated his life to intellectual distance.

Another spin an actor might take would flip which motive was conscious and unconscious. If revenge is seen through a Christian lens, then "to avenge my father by killing his murderer" is a mortal sin that Hamlet knows he is committing to, and "to seek any justification to save my soul from damnation" would be the unconscious or semi-conscious tugging of Hamlet's better angels. †

When a character is thinking rationally and productively, they will lean into their conscious, usually nobler objective. As they feel vulnerable, insecure, and emotional, they lean back into a reactive mode. If we analyze a character's journey through a play in this way, we might think of them as if they are walking a tightrope between virtue and vice, between growth and regression. The audience cheers when they make progress across that rope, and we wince when they turn back or falter.

The actor can benefit by thinking of their journey as a series of steps forward or backward pulled as they are between these two poles. This can also help a director shape a scene as they highlight those moments when a character is pulled between their competing objectives. The choices made in such moments are the substance of the plot.

The Inevitability of Free Will

I have been speaking mainly from the perspective of narrative drama. There are of course many forms of theatre that move away from the typical presentation of story, character, and theme. I sense, however, that character—the presentation of the human on stage caught on the tightrope of choice—is fairly consistent across experimental theatrical forms, right up into dance's territory.

† This take may go against the play's overall signaling. Although Shakespeare wrote many plays with Christian values at their core, *Hamlet* does not seem to be one of them. Horatio's "flights of angels sing thee to thy rest" speech is spoken as if Hamlet has achieved his moral victory in finally exacting justice on Claudius.

A performer walks onstage. We assume there is a need that has brought them here. Almost as if they are fated for free will. Theatre—our sacred space—is a celebration and a memorial of humanity thrust into the world fated for free will.

Plays, and stories generally, enact both fate and free will simultaneously. A character in crisis with a need to respond chooses a course of action, and the audience perceives thereby their moral makeup. We only see one choice play out, and that choice leads to a clear outcome. And so it feels like fate. Like history. But a play is a living thing when you read it and when you see it. So it feels, in the moment, like free will playing out, morphing into fate. Like wet cement that becomes hardened. Set in stone.

Trying to separate the two starts to feel like pretzel logic. Or perhaps, thinking more holistically, we are trying to separate yin and yang. Some plays, however, through their thematic treatment, emphasize predestination and others amplify human choice. The work of Bertolt Brecht and Augusto Boal are examples of the latter, while the Greeks and the Absurdists presented the former.

My suggestion is that even when fate weighs heavily, we look for the range of choice. A character facing terminal cancer does not have the power to will themself to health, but they may have the time to choose how they will face their end. Two tramps stuck in a wasteland cannot force a neglectful universe to answer their needs, but they can determine whether they will face that universe together or alone.

Part Three

Community

13

Faltering and Recovering

I have doubted people. Early on I learned to mistrust people or maybe to trust them only so far, and my experience throughout life has both confirmed and challenged that. I never doubted myself though. As a child I was mostly raised by my mother, and one of her greatest gifts was not just her love but her belief in me. And so it was much easier for me to absorb that belief.

That belief carried me through my 20s, when I did not doubt the viability or necessity to get a B.A. and M.F.A. in theatre arts. In my 30s and 40s, I struggled in my career as a playwright to find traction and build momentum. I attribute this to failing to establish any fully-fledged creative partnerships, which as I've mentioned are essential to flourishing as a theatre artist. Still my life was fulfilling in many ways, I had a good job in my field, and I was blessed to be engaged in community building activities. So, despite my lack of professional success, I continued to muster belief in myself and keep going as a writer.

Until five years ago. And then the bottom fell out of my self-confidence. I got to a point where continuing with playwriting seemed simply insane. I was getting very few productions or even readings, and the ones I got sometimes felt embarrassing because of how tepid audience turnout was. My plays may have had value, but even my friends showed little interest.

On June 23, amid a season of depression, I wrote the following in my journal:

> *"Another night of not enough sleep. I'm up late in a state of existential bewilderment. A phrase came to me that is like a breeze of relief: 'I am retiring from playwriting.'*
>
> *"25 years was a good go of it, but the past dozen or so years have brought simply frustration."*

And so I stopped writing plays. At 51.

Call it a midlife crisis, but it hit me where my heart was. This had been my calling, the way I would contribute my gift to the world. But the world didn't want this gift from me. What is a gift if you force it on someone? It's a burden.

So it was up to me to let go, release all that psychic energy that had been concentrated in dozens of plays with decades of work poured into them. This was no small step, but it felt freeing and necessary. I made no announcement. I realized that would just be a plea for encouragement, and I was beyond that point. If someone brought up my writing or my connection to theatre, I might talk about it. But for the most part, people didn't.

Looking for the Disconnect

There are a lot of reasons I can give for the disconnect between my playwriting and potential collaborators. This includes, most obviously, the limitations of my writing, but I do see work produced that my work is at least on par with, objectively speaking. But I'd like to explore a few other reasons because I think they relate to others' experience or to larger trends.

First is the level of interest. Collaborators need to be enthusiastic enough about your work to actively step forward and do it. This ties to subject and treatment and whether people see themselves in the work. Do actors start imagining what it would be like to play the role? Are designers thinking about possibilities of set or costume or lighting? Is a director struck with the impact of the play such that they want to be the contractor that turns the blueprint into a building? I recognize now how much of a writer's success ties to writing at a wavelength that people are already tuned into. Interest also follows social trends and young energy.

The second reason is people are busy. Theatre makers schedule themselves way in advance, a year or more sometimes. New work is green and budding and needs attention when it is developing or else it withers. Theatre folk have to find regular jobs because they need to live and have health care, so they may be enthusiastic about a piece, but time is precious. Add small children, and it becomes almost unfeasible, and there go all your friends and colleagues in their 30s and 40s. Overworked and distracted, who has time to challenge the status quo?

The third reason I'd add is our era of hesitancy with commitment and relationship. I have been baffled by how many potential collaborations have just dissolved because individuals perceive some difference of viewpoint or a possible imperfection. Rather than work through it, they just abandoned the project. To be fair this has been less the case with professional theatre folk than civilians stepping into the role of producer. (Because my work borders community building, I am often working with people from outside our trade.)

In theatre we learn a lesson that much of the rest of the world doesn't yet understand. When collaborators have different perspectives, this doesn't necessitate compromise. That is a zero-sum mindset. No, when collaborators enter into a project in good faith and with different views, we work through the differences and often arrive at a solution that transcends either individual's original view. This is an abundance mindset in practice.

One other possible explanation of the disconnect was that I was being punished by fate or divine displeasure for some past or present sin, and so my career was confounded in some Babel-esque confusion among collaborators. I do not dismiss this outright as a possibility, but it is not exactly actionable outside penitence and penance.

So at age 51 and 52, I started to consider a career pivot. Maybe a Ph.D.? I didn't really see myself as a dramaturg or historian, but I felt if I didn't find something to pursue and to feel good about, I was opening myself up to sickness.

Drama Circle

A little over a year into my "retirement", I was having coffee with Hannah, a former student of mine who had recently graduated, and we got on the topic of our connection to theatre. Even before arriving at college, she had been passionate about directing. Now after being out of school for only a few months, this bright young theatre artist was already feeling some dimming of her enthusiasm and connection to theatre. Something was lacking in the theatre scene she was finding, an energy that she had perhaps taken for granted at university.

After graduating, Hannah had gotten a job with the same charter high school she had attended before coming to UNC. It was there she had been mentored by one of those doggedly dedicated and largely unsung heroes that are high school theatre teachers. Hannah was working in the school office, helping to organize student testing by day, and in the evenings and weekends she was working as an assistant director with some local theatre companies.

For my part, I opened up and shared with her my disillusionment and retirement from playwriting. Although I refrained from speaking about this with students in my classes, she was now a young colleague out in the world. Anyway, a wounded person can hardly open their mouth without giving away their pain.

We discussed revitalizing our connection to theatre—resuscitating might have been the word for me. I later invited her to have dinner with me and Azi at our home. That night we talked about starting a group, inviting some handpicked people to get together and try to reclaim the vital and urgent connection we formerly felt with our art form. We would call it "drama circle," the name of the dormant theatre company I had started twenty years earlier. Hannah typed up our ideas in bullet point form:

Drama Circle

- *To build/enjoy community without pressure to produce*
- *To rediscover some spark/joy/power/holiness of theatre*
- *To collectively determine what the world needs from theatre right now…or maybe just what we need from theatre right now…*
- *To share and explore words that excite and move us forward*

We would host it at our home. We could meet out on our stage-like patio, which just so happens to be a circle. When the weather wasn't so nice, we could meet in our living room. The space didn't matter as much as the intention.

We invited friends and colleagues who seemed to be of like mind. I found it appealed less to my busy colleagues than to former students. We met—just a handful of people, and it was beautiful. We began with dinner, then we moved to a time for sharing a poem, a scene, a monologue, or a song. What people shared was heartfelt, and the responses were thoughtful and entirely positive without feigning. I pulled out a scene I had written a long while ago. Then we had tea and dessert and we talked and laughed. The room had been rarefied through the sharing of the sacred fire that is art. It was no matter that we were a small group. People left recharged, feeling happy and welcome to come back next time.

We held the gathering again about a month later. Then again. And again. The composition switched around a bit. Some of the same folks came back, some new people joined. I continued sharing work I'd previously written. The group stayed at an intimate size, where we could all still squeeze around the dinner table.

We started coming up with themes for people to write towards, if they so desired. A couple people would write scenes, more seemed to gravitate towards poetry. One time Hannah and the group decided that I specifically should write a five-minute standup comedy piece. I had only written one or two new things since the group started, but I took the challenge. I ended up writing a half-hour long monologue called "Careful Not to Laugh," a piece about death and legacy and how perfectionism can result from subpar parenting.

The effect it had on the group was surprising. It was one of the strongest reactions I'd ever had to my writing, even if it was only 4 or 5 people there to hear it. This was the most playwriting I had done in 2 years, and I had spent maybe a week of evenings working on it. I allowed myself no greater ambition than to gift it to the people who were present that evening. In that regard, it had been a complete success, and that was enough.

From that night, my two-year retirement from playwriting ended. I started to write again, albeit only for drama circle. And I found that time had not degraded my skill, as it might if I were a concert musician, but it seemed to come back a little stronger, at least in some ways.

Forgetting Love and Remembering it Again

An evening of scenes and poetry.

07.21.24

6:30PM Potluck// 8PM Show

We have continued the group for almost four years now, with several of the same folks as were there that first time. Many others have passed in and out, and they are still considered part of our circle. One summer we featured some performances of our work and invited folks to come see our work performed around our drama circle stage. Otherwise, it's been dinner, sharing, and tea, and a commitment to rekindling our love for theatre and art with no regard for audience-pleasing or money-making.

I am writing again. No, I am not immune from the same frustrations that ground me down to dust last time. I am learning, however, to let go of expectations about reception. I strive now to write for the love of the work and for the sharing of that work to as many as are there and want to listen. The sacredness of an action has never been about crowd size. As Jesus said, "For where two or three gather in my name, there am I with them."

Choosing Community

Hannah has remained an integral member of our drama circle. This was a welcome surprise. I had assumed she would go off to New York or to an M.F.A. graduate program in directing at Yale or Northwestern. From the first time I met her in a first-year seminar full of STEM majors and undecided folks, she stuck out. The class—called 'The Heart of the Play' is geared as a soft entry to our art, so I felt from the beginning her chomping on the bit, wanting more intensity, more depth, more specifics.

But this was not the sort of class where some who are gifted or special get to shine brighter while others recede into passivity. The approach of the class was holistic. It's not that "I go far"; it's that "we go together". And that approach sunk in for her. In her graduation speech four years later, she spoke of this idea of the "heart" and making sure it was first.

Hannah has remained working for her high school, but she has since moved from the office to the theatre classroom, where she has replaced her mentor who retired. She is the school's theatre teacher.

When she first mentioned this possibility, I was a bit baffled. Are you sure? Again, in my mind, I had plugged her into a more ambitious career track. I mean teaching high school theatre is unrelenting. That's the front lines. But she was sure. She liked teaching. Most of all, she cared about this community. Why would she go and look for another one to serve when she already was integrated here?

The student had surpassed the teacher.

14

Reframing

Theatre does not need to follow one path. There are many ways it may be integrated into our lives and our communities. If you find yourself working among caring collaborators and making meaningful art, this is a blessing. By all means, ride that train till the last station.

If, on the other hand, you find yourself isolated and unable to engage meaningfully with the art you love to do, it may be time to reframe. If you find yourself bereft of community, it may be necessary to build it.

Start small. An orchard begins with saplings, or seedlings even. After that, it's just about time and attention and care. These are the constants in this sacred work.

One simple suggestion I offer is holding a 'drama circle' or similar gathering. Invite people together with the intention of sharing art and hospitality. If people aren't ready to write their own pieces, you can read other people's work: plays or monologues or scenes, poems, maybe passages from prose.

Sing songs. Paint or sculpt or knit. All arts are sacred, and all arts are meant to foster community.

The future of the arts, like the future of business and other civic institutions, may benefit greatly from some decentering. Our reliance on national models has a disempowering effect on our local engagement and initiative. Rather than watch, let us perform. Rather than listen, let us sing. Rather than scroll down, let us rise up and do.

New Work

Consider a lesson from the natural world: A tree uses half of the energy it produces through photosynthesis for maintenance and the other half for growth. Imagine if half the energy of the theatre world went into new work. And imagine if, just like a tree, the growth were spread out throughout the boughs and branches of the theatre world.

Now that's an ambitious vision. That would mean local and regional theatre companies, high schools and universities, community theatres and art centers—all could host sessions encouraging people to write or devise work. Not necessarily for production, but for the enjoyment among those present. And many are currently offering this.

For playwriting, the needed resources are minimal—paper and pencils, chairs and tables, some basic writing prompts, and an instructor who mainly acts by encouraging. Have people write for 15-20 minutes. Then you go around and everyone can share what they've written with feedback afterwards or not. There's just something about being heard, something fundamentally healing.

With devised work, the resources may even be more minimal. You need space and people. Throw in some chairs and tables, and you open some possibilities of levels. Throw in a few props, and you add distinct story indicators. Here the instructor will probably need some training, but essentially the goal is to craft a story through the ideas of the group. And the healing factor here is the invigoration of the collective melding of hearts and minds. When imaginations start overlapping and the sparks of ideas start to fly, laughter and delight emerge, but also perhaps sorrow or solemnity.

Our sacred space is not reserved for finished work. It is available all the way through the process. Of course, I've described here the very earliest steps of new play development. Next steps include revising work, holding more formal readings, workshopping ideas, and of course mounting production at whatever scale.

To continue the analogy of a tree's growth, we may think of this local level of theatrical work as the leaves that cover the tree. It's the means of gathering all the energy, which then enables the production of the fine fruits. The mature work of a theatrical cycle will come in its own time, but there is always important work to be done in our sacred space.

In thinking about where theatre and playwriting are today, I have come to focus my thinking on a few overlapping areas that I find promising in the development of new work. The first, as anachronistic as it might sound, is folk drama.

Recalling Folk Traditions

When I go to the theatre, I love nothing more than being introduced to a richly depicted world different than the one I know, but made familiar through the people who I come to care for by seeing them engage wholeheartedly in a struggle suitable to their environment.

I am thinking of that luxuriant first act of *Intimate Apparel* by Lynn Nottage, where we are introduced to Esther, a black seamstress, who labors to live and love in New York in 1905. She has these sweet, intimate interactions with the Hasidic fabric salesman. Watching those scenes, my heart was about to burst for love of my kind.

What was the secret of that play's effect on me? It could come down to form, but I believe it was love. Love begets love. Lynn Nottage was writing about her great-grandmother.

A century ago, the University of North Carolina had a critical role in the development and spread of a distinctive approach to playwriting. Professor Frederick Koch and the Carolina Playmakers fostered a little, local revolution by turning their energies onto "folk" drama. This would have repercussions far beyond Chapel Hill as the influence of the Carolina Playmakers spread in the first half of the 20th Century. "Proff" Koch describes it thus:

> *From the first our particular interest in North Carolina has been the use of native materials and the making of fresh dramatic forms. We have found that if the young writer observes the locality with which he is most familiar and interprets it faithfully it may show him the way to the universal. If he can see the interestingness of the lives of those about him with understanding and imagination, with wonder, why may he not interpret that life in significant images for others—perhaps for all? It has been so in all lasting art.*

The materials were drawn by each writer from scenes familiar and near, often from remembered adventures of his youth, from folk tales and the common tradition, and from present-day life. [1]

The impact of folk traditions has shifted greatly in the modern age because of the relentless homogenization of culture in the electronic age. The basic notion, however, that we belong to certain groups with certain world views and certain lived experiences is still quite true. That perspective of the world is a treasure one can share.

I have students who feel quite isolated and distinctly not part of a "folk tradition", and then I ask them to dig a little deeper. They end up writing a scene that wows the class with its unique and nuanced picture of a setting so different from the ones the rest of us know.

If we start with this conception of "folk"—either the people we come from or those we gravitate towards, we find certain communities that we know well. We have some sense of belonging or trust or even obligation to this community, however, large or small. It might be an ethnic grouping, a neighborhood or locale, a common identity, a vocation, a certain club, or simply a unique group of friends.

There is rich dramatic potential in the environments we may take for granted. Ultimately, a play is about people, but there is much to be said about place and culture and feel that adds freshness and resonance to a story. If we approach this sharing of our little world to the larger world in the proper spirit, it is a sacred act. And hearts will be opened.

---

[1] Frederick Koch, *American Folk Plays*. New York: Appleton-Century, 1939. pp. xiv-xv

Writing for an Intended Audience

Many writers begin with the question, "What do I want to write about?" or "What story is bubbling up inside of me?" Some might be more utilitarian and ask, "What do I need to write about to get the attention of theatre producers?"

An alternative is to take inspiration from theatre artists who work closely with their communities and who start with the question, "What does my community need?" Here we are thinking from the perspective of theatre as medicine.

The same way we have our communities and our "folk" that we may write about, we may also write <u>for</u> such communities or such settings. The fundamental questions then become: "What communities am I part of? Who are my folk—the ones I know well enough to make art for? What kind of imbalances do we perceive in those spaces? What kind of dramatic event can we bring that will be like medicine?"

This approach can work equally well for a play written by an individual and for a collaboratively devised work. The way this differs from the way art is generally conceived is that the creative seed is not just found within oneself or the group, but in the contemplation of the needs of others.

And as I mentioned in an earlier chapter, we are not out to fix the problems of others. We reflect in our hearts and consult with others. What can we bring to that group that would enrich them, or heal them, or provoke them, or edify them, or simply bring them the joy of light entertainment? It might be a full performance or just a reading.

We could make a comic piece sending up the personalities in a close-knit group to make everyone laugh. We could make a deeply moving ritualistic piece meant to tap into a common spiritual belief. We could dramatize an historical event to educate and bring a stronger sense of common bond in the group. We could put on a provocation to awaken complacent people from their slumber.

I don't believe that this act of intentional writing or devising needs to be cerebral or approached outwardly. One may decide to be deliberate and work out a need, a method, and a plan before creating the piece. One may also work on it more intuitively, creating as one reflects on the community and its needs. It is also not necessarily in conflict with autobiographical impulses. One may find a balance here between writing for others and writing from oneself.

The big idea is to find purpose in aiming our craft not towards a general audience, but to one that we already have bonds and ties with, one where we start from a position of care.

One Act Plays with Post Show Discussions

Just as there is a need to decenter the western dramatic canon, there is a need to decenter the full-length play.

The full-length play may be understood as a commercial creation. It is meant to provide a complete cycle through emotion and to create a sense of holistic vicarious experience. It lasts about as long as human attention can be effectively sustained. When it's done and the lights go up, you've got your feelings but you're basically ready to go home. Theatres know that holding talkbacks after long plays is a hard sell. The vast majority of the audience heads for the doors.

Not so with a one-act.

When you see a short play and the lights go up, the experience feels unfinished. When I've presented shorter works without much attention to talkbacks, I've found audiences just aren't ready to go home. They hang out, seek out actors, and talk with other audience members. The play has successfully opened them up, but they don't feel the closure yet.

This signals to me an opportunity for social action and civic engagement. Some companies out there have beat me to this question, but here is a framing of it: What if we cultivate a species of one-act play that thoughtfully raises a topic of social import but does not resolve it? Then what if we allow the audience, representatives of the greater community, to grapple with the questions raised? We would need a capable moderator to ask questions and move the conversation along, but not to provide answers. We also don't necessarily need a panel telling us the answers. That would be a different kind of effort. Here, in our age of isolation and siloed information streams, an open conversation is the point.

I have written a few such plays and the effect can be quite potent. This scenario seems most successful to me when the play is almost entirely forgotten except as a reference point to the conversation about the real world. Someone may eventually ask an actor how they memorized all those lines, but that is less likely with a 45-minute-long play.

We all love full-length plays. I am not making a call to eliminate them. I offer this model, however, in consideration of giving theatre a more active role in awakening societal conversation and providing space for civic dialogue.

15

Our Production of *The Seagull*

There is new work, and there is the library of that which came before. Like all theatre people, I love much of that library and much of the dramatic canon. As a theatre educator, I feel it's partly my responsibility to be a custodian and curator of that library. At one point, I was using a certain rating system in my recommendations, especially of older plays. The system basically boiled down to the following categories: AVOID IT, READ IT, SEE IT, STUDY IT, and STAGE IT. This was my estimation of how much time a particular script was worth for students.

In the contemporary world, even some of the best work from the past might not quite reach the STAGE IT category. A lot about that work is problematic given current sensibilities and at the very least requires a feminist or decolonizing lens in staging. To call back a play vital in my journey, it makes a difference in *My Fair Lady* if Eliza is standing boldly between Higgins and Pickering as they sing "You did it" versus if she is moping in a chair to the side.

One play I adore but did not wish to stage was *The Seagull* by Anton Chekhov. I told our director of undergraduate production this when he floated the idea.

"Dave, we all love *The Seagull.* It's Chekhov, it's about theatre people, it's got a play within a play. But it ends with the suicide of one young, struggling artist and the psychological evisceration of another! This happens while the older, successful artists play games and eat a pleasant supper. The message is clear: there is not enough room for the young in the arts, because the older generation won't make room for them!"

"Yeah, but the students want to do it."

"Why on earth—as an artist-educator who is seeking to train and encourage young artists—would I purposefully choose to produce with those young people and for other young people a play which is telling them there is no hope for you in the world of the arts, because the older generation is too greedy and self-centered to let you in?"

"I don't know, Mark, but you're my Chekhov guy."

I do include Chekhov in a couple of my classes, and I had directed a production of *The Cherry Orchard* several years before. Actually, I had done a special topics course in the fall on Chekhov and then directed the play in spring. It was part of an effort in our department to connect the classroom with student productions, and it was quite successful. The students came away with an impressive understanding of the shifting nature of Chekhovian drama, and then they succeeded to embody that concept onstage in that sublime play.

Well, despite my misgivings, we went ahead with *The Seagull,* and my plan was to somehow deconstruct that despairing message and instead communicate a message of empowerment. We again would take the fall semester to dedicate to understanding Chekhov and this play and then perform the play in late February. The syllabus would be similar to the one I used for *The Cherry Orchard* class some years before. We would read Chekhov's plays, some short stories, and some scholarship around his dramaturgy. His is not a self-evident performance style, even as Impressionism is not a self-evident approach to painting.

Looking around at the class on the first day, I was delighted. This was a special group. They were mostly seniors—the Class of 2024, which meant this group had entered at the height of COVID. Their first year of college was on Zoom, when they should have been socializing, finding friend groups, and exercising their fledgling independence. Their mental health—and that of most other students—began to decay. This flared up when they came back in the fall of 2021. The university was pushing normalcy with masks, and things were not normal. The students were anxious and depressed. They were angry, and they felt isolated from other students, mistrustful of university administration, and doubtful of the purpose of this education of theirs. It was when they started jumping off the roofs of the dorms mid-semester that the University started paying real attention. O my goodness, what we have done to our young people!

So the class of 2024 faced special challenges with social connections. Not so this group! The students I had around me had fought their way through their mental health challenges back into the theatre. They had started with plays on Zoom and, when live performance started back up, they jumped into auditioning like it was a lifeline. They helped the juniors and seniors resurrect the many student theatre groups. They overextended themselves trying to make up for lost stage time. And by their senior year, this cohort, which could have been handicapped by circumstance, had seized the reins of their artistic agency. They sat now, eager to extract that nectar of mystery that seeps from the work of Anton Chekhov.

Confronting the Gun

I began the class with a question: How do we tell this story in such a way that we do not damage or discourage the young artists who are in it or who see it? The play can be changed. It's public domain. Chekhov will survive. We can make choices about the stories we choose to tell.

Not everyone in the class was sold on the idea of messing with Chekhov's gun, so to speak. But there was enough goodwill to proceed, and we jumped that first week into a lively reading of the play. With the amount of commentary and questions, it became clear that they were loving the play and that we would not finish reading the play in the two class periods in our Tues/Thurs schedule. No worries, we'd pick it up the following Tuesday.

Then on Monday at 1:03 pm, sirens started wailing. The UNC community received a text that there was a lockdown for an active shooter. For three hours, students, staff, and faculty cowered in classrooms, offices and closets waiting for word, listening for doors opening and footsteps approaching, scrolling furiously for information, texting with others, sharing unfounded rumors amid the vacuum left by university authorities.

We later learned a graduate student had killed a Chemistry professor over in Caudill Labs and had fled the building and was at large for some time before being caught. We were in the national news.

When we returned to class on Thursday, the question of the inevitability of Chekhov's gun had been reframed. Some of these students had harrowing experiences waiting for the all clear. For all, the lockdown had magnified feelings of anxiety, lack of control, and general disillusionment.

We took time to work through the feelings and eventually finished our reading of the play. There it was, the gun shot that rings out and spoils the party. What do we do about that? Then we had a 2nd lockdown because of an armed individual only two weeks after the first.

How do we change this narrative? It wasn't just about the guns; it's about the sense that your autonomy has been taken away from you by a society that has already decided everything; they've mapped the world, exploited its treasures, curated its chosen artifacts, disrupted its critical ecological balance, poured concrete and despair into every available crevice where a young person might incline to set their own foundation.

I was more certain than ever of my central purpose here. As the older artist in this room, I needed to do the opposite of what the older artists in the play do. I needed to get out of the way, empower these young artists, lift them up so their decisions were centered, their creativity recognized. They needed to feel heard and valued, not just for what they contributed, but for who they were before they did a single thing. Where scarcity pervades the play, we would have abundance. Where Kostya and Nina felt the need to prove themselves, we would trust that the capacity was already there.

If we were to really address the play's fatalism, we needed to investigate, not just the behavior of Arkadina and Trigorin, but how I as professor and director would share space with these students. This is when I came across the right message at the right moment.

A Model of "Narrative Justice Playmaking"

A colleague in the building had forwarded a podcast transcript from UC Berkley's *Berkley Voices*[2] about an innovative approach to theatre emphasizing social justice and what seemed like a radical inclusiveness. A new professor there, Timmia Hearn DeRoy, was sharing an approach to what she called "narrative justice playmaking", which centers the emancipation and self-actualization of performers and audience. It's modeled on Carnival from Trinidad and Tobago, and I was especially struck by the example she gave of her COVID-time production of *Everybody* by Branden Jacobs Jenkins, where she said:

> *"[T]he whole production (of Everybody) was designed around: How can we generate collective healing around the collective loss that we've experienced? And also: How can we train our*

[2] Anne Brice, "Theatre as Power: New professor brings Caribbean performance practice to Berkley", *Berkley Voices.* October 17, 2023.

students, because it was a university production, to share power?"

So instead of the play having a random lottery for who will play the roles—including the Everybody character doomed to die, she had the audience voting. And what happened was that the actors started rallying the audience to vote for their colleagues to make sure each got to play the lead role.

"[A]ll of the students who participated in this project left this project understanding what power-sharing means, having participated and made their own decisions to share power and to advocate for others to share power … And because everyone felt so invested in the collective of this production, there was this sense of unity, there was this sense of love, there was this sense of standing up for each other."

Hallelujah, this was what I wanted for our company. This was transformational.

The class continued, and we made our way through the plays and the scholarship., but I found even as we refined our understanding of how to perform Chekhov, I was more conscious than ever of the need to remake the established power dynamics of both the classroom and the rehearsal room. It wasn't just about what we put onstage. A philosophy needed to be integrated throughout the entire process.

The ideas I had about abundance and purpose and community were coalescing into a practice. I was trying to listen more, trusting the students' instincts, finding opportunities to let them lead. They were reading the same material I was, or they were researching topics I might not know about. I didn't need to be the expert on everything. I needed to be a facilitator for the emerging ideas and just keep the project on track.

Taking Flight and Some Turbulence

In November, we were set to hold auditions. Most of the class was intending to audition; a few were wanting to work on technical or production team assignments. The goal of the class had been to create a core ensemble with a collective understanding of how to approach the play. Taking the class did not guarantee you the role you wanted, but you would get a role.

Chekhov's play has ten significant roles, four women and six men. I think we had eight young women from the class alone auditioning! (This is not to mention those auditioning who weren't in the class.) We also, like every other college these days, have a strong gender disparity in available actors. We needed a fix in the key of abundance.

One simple decision was to cast cross-gender for certain roles. That was agreeable to the group. Another decision was double casting, especially for main roles. This wasn't universally applauded, but the necessity did occur to folks.

For auditions, I invited those students from the class who were not auditioning to come sit with me and watch. Several did, and we made decisions together. We welcomed the majority of those who auditioned to callbacks.

For callbacks, we had students work in pairs with sides from the show. Everyone would be assigned a scene, they'd go rehearse for 15-20 minutes, then they'd come back and we would all watch one another's work and applaud when they finished. This was not about outdoing or outpacing one another. This was like a two evening Chekhov acting course. It was an end in itself. I shared at the end how grateful I was for the encouraging and communal environment they had created. The great majority of those in that room would become part of the company, either cast or crew.

The day after callbacks, we had a scheduled quiz in the Chekhov class. I gave the students their quiz paper and when they finished with that, I handed them the second part of the quiz. It was a list of the roles in *The Seagull* and the names of all those at callbacks. I asked them, with the 15 minutes remaining in the class, to cast the show (or rather to double cast it!) based on what they had seen. Not as a group, but as individuals.

Oh, they howled and complained! They hated the idea and loved it at the same time. But they did it. And I went through all their answers, marked them on a whiteboard. Oh, it was a mess, but in the end, I took about two-thirds of the cast list from their top few picks.

The final cast list consisted of 20 people. I passed it by a couple of the non-acting members of the class, who concurred. Five main roles were double cast, five other roles were single cast, and five other roles would be ensemble. The ensemble was especially to integrate a cohort of first-year students who showed promise and who have since become major contributors in our building. Dave wasn't super happy about me creating a need to costume 20 people for a 10 person play, but I was determined.

Some of the choices were a bit controversial. Casting a first-year student not in the class as one of the Ninas enraged one member of the class so much she chose not to accept a role as Paulina. Everyone else came on board. I should mention that first year student had been one of the top picks of the class, not just mine.

To be fair, the dual role of teacher and director is problematic. A teacher's role is to treat all students equally and help lift each to the next stage of their development. Any sign of favoritism is a breach. A director that makes a cast list has already crossed that threshold. If I take on this teacher-director role again, I will need to consider another approach for casting.

Decentering the Director, Maintaining the Direction

Over the winter break, I reflected on a thesis and I will share it at the end of this chapter. You will notice it reads almost like a synopsis of this book.

In January, we set off on one of the most profound rehearsal processes I and the company members had experienced. It was the form of it. I will not take the time to go minutely through the creative choices we made. I will just share the big decisions, especially those that ran contrary to my directing training from back in undergrad.

- The primary staging method we used was the same I discovered in callbacks. Take one scene and give it to two different groups, send them off for 15-20 minutes, bring them both back and have them perform for everyone. Since the main roles were double cast and we had ensemble members, we could do this. We then would take the best ideas from both scenes, block the scene, and move on. It wasn't a competition either. The complementarity of the two scenes was always striking.

- While they were off rehearsing their scenes, I would make tea for everyone. I brought in a samovar from our home and made Persian tea. (The samovar happens to be a typical Chekhovian prop.) The cast and crew loved the tea, and the fact that I made it emphasized the role of hospitality in our production. We would eventually transfer this job to the stage management team, and they would prepare tea in the samovar for our audience. Yes, we gave tea and sugar cookies to our audience.
- The staging would be in the round, and the set would be basically a large turntable we repurposed from PlayMakers' production of *Misery*. Unlike that production, our turntable would be manually operated. It would represent the wheel of Fortune, the comings and goings of life, the change of seasons, etc. Actors would spin it between acts as we played out dream segments involving the characters.
- The ensemble, everyone in fact, would be angels. They have come here tonight to share a cautionary tale with us about choosing scarcity over abundance, selfishness over love. This idea bubbled up as we considered the influence of the Symbolist movement on Chekhov and the arts of his time. The play begins with all twenty appearing suddenly around the theatre, somber for the story they tell. They come together into a circle and choose who will tell the story that night. Half take on the burden of these

roles, while the rest watch with clear eyes and empathy. They come off and on throughout the show as a chorus, as the ideal Chekhovian audience.

- The biggest ask I made was regarding the way the double-cast actors would choose who performed which night. This hearkened back to Timmia DeRoy's work with *Everybody*. I asked the pairs to work out between themselves which night they wished to perform, but not to tell anyone else. Of course these were the main roles, so what nights your family and friends come is at stake. What I wanted to avoid was any sense of purposeful alignment (of friends, say), because it seemed to go against the spirit of our collective. In the rehearsal process, the fluidity with which all the combinations worked with each other was spectacular. And this was repeated in performance. We had different arrangements of performers every night, so every show was different.

Working on *The Seagull* with this company was a blessed experience, and the quality of the show reflected the process. The actors' absorption in the story was enchanting, and their care for one another was palpable. I would just watch mesmerized as the angel that, for example, played the double for Konstantine watched with great care over the one who was "on" that night as he struggled with the belief that nobody cared. The angels remade the play but didn't say a word.

A couple weeks after the show closed, we had the cast and crew to our home for spaghetti and meatballs. It was a lovely night, and after dinner we talked about the process and product. I asked them how they would articulate the experience. I felt we needed to articulate it to transfer some of these lessons we learned to other scenarios. The students were effusive in their gratitude for the whole process, for the sense of trust and empowerment they felt. The overarching theme of abundance really hit home for them, tea and all.

The Seagull Directing Thesis

"The Seagull can be understood as an inevitability or a cautionary tale. Artists and writers don't have to scrape and tussle in a desperate attempt to secure attention in a zero-sum game. Art is sacred and therefore can open up into abundance if one doesn't make it a vehicle simply of self and ambition. In the act of creation, the connection between artist and audience is the essential one, esp. when the result is Uplift and the infusion of the Sublime and the Beautiful. Fame and fortune do not bring happiness although they cast a spell that can be mistaken for it.

"Love is not a zero-sum game either. Like fame and fortune, it too can be mistaken for happiness. But love only brings happiness when it is freed from a deep-rooted insecurity and mistaken placement.

"In love and art, one must guard against scarcity mentality; rather one should expect and embrace abundance. Love is not the same thing as attraction and success in art is not conditioned on acquiring fame and fortune.

"The young are especially harmed in an environment where insecurity and scarcity reign.

"Abundance is scary sometimes. In the overwhelmed heart, the inundated mind, abundance bubbles up like boiling water, creating motion where it's never been before."

Abundance

There is enough time.

There is enough space.

There is enough warmth.

There is enough food and water.

There is enough light.

There is enough love to go around.

There is someone for everyone.

Any melody can have a harmony to enrich it.

Opportunities for necessary interactions will come ...
in due time.

I can flourish with the opportunities that open up for me.

Art will find its audience.

How can one compare with Nature as to artistry?
Or to the Heart for compulsion and drive?

The earth can heal itself.

Trauma doesn't injure your essence.

Crisis is the spirit's beckoning.

Problems create an opening for growth
on a level higher than the problem itself.

Sharing your feelings can unblock the avenue of the heart
and allow relationships to grow,
rebuild or improve.

Genius is accessible to us. But one must understand it
as a drawing on a deeper source.

Excellence can be an outcome of abundance,
when natural talent is refined through
discipline and openness.

Detachment from the fruits of abundance is essential
if one is to remain in it.

Love is a seed that will grow.

Listening is an expression of love.

Unlike attraction, Love is tested in letting go.

Gratitude is the proper response to abundance.

16

Conclusion

I have said a lot to you who read these words, you who are my collaborators in the sacred work. I guess what I have to say to the Theatre is the same thing a lover would write in a love song or a love letter:

You broke my heart, but I love you still.

Now how do we go forward from here?

Does theatre need a resurrection? Well, civilization certainly needs a resurrection, but the theatre is our charge. I have striven to include in this little book the big ideas that I have come to believe are some essentials in our improvement.

Abundance. Purpose. Community. I guess these are the core ideas. And sacredness, of course. Without that, our work is disconnected from its power source.

Sacred space restores.

Sacred space heals.

Sacred space finds the right medicine for the time.

Sacred space confronts.

Sacred space bends.

We lighten or we dim, we consecrate or we desecrate the space with our approach and our intention.

When we share stories that awaken awareness, when we engage in our duties in a wholehearted way, when we resist outmoded hierarchies, when we choose to believe in people, we are bringing the remedy to an ailing world.

The sun is risen, and the light is waiting to break forth from behind these dark clouds. The day is in motion and the heat is climbing. The problems are many and bewildering, but the approaches we need are available.

None of us can do it alone. And that's the point.

We must learn to work together. This is the secret hidden in plain sight. This is our salvation and our solace.

Whether it's neighbors of different races, citizens of different political persuasions, or nations locked in entrenched patterns of mistrust and intimidation—we are a single planet, a magical glistening pearl spinning in space teeming with life and possibility.

This earth is our sacred space. We can do our part to restore it. Our theatre work may seem small in comparison, but we can contribute to this grand realignment. I pray that you may feel empowered in your task and hopeful in your heart.

This Sacred Space

My Teachers

I began this book, this manifesto-memoir, with a dedication to my students, and now I end it with a word of gratitude for my teachers, many of whom have transitioned from this life. I will list some of them here:

From Bob Jordan, I learned the transformative possibilities of verbalizing the evident.

From Tom Meehan, I learned the effect of feeling seen and valued by someone I respected.

From Thomas Smith, I learned I had Peter Pan syndrome and the value of cutting through the nonsense.

From Christine St. Jean, I learned the empowering impact of allowing a student time to find their words.

From David Avcollie, I learned that a humble posture magnifies the power of attention.

From Michael Sokoloff, I learned humility: "Not quite, Mr. Perry ... But it's good for you."

From Mary Ann Bentley, I learned the essential role of welcoming young people into theatre space.

From Nancy Cole, I learned a gentle, yet enthusiastic approach to theatre history.

From Chris Steele, I learned the self-assurance to communicate an artistic vision.

From Denis Calandra, I learned the dialect of the Bard and now he is a friend and no stranger.

From Pat Finelli, I learned that deep academic discussions are best held in an informal, collegial environment.

From Paul Massie, I learned ... oh, Paul ... I learned the difference it makes when your teacher loves you.

From Art Borreca, I learned to hold a space for artists where all are uplifted with the least possible force.

From Dare Clubb, I learned the joy of condensing more and more life and truth into the work.

From Kim Marra, I learned the charm of understatement in a lecture and the resulting dynamic opportunity for truth to ring the louder.

From Alan MacVey, I witnessed a model of artistic and academic excellence, high efficiency, and basic decency.

From Sydné Mahone, I found a model of reading the work of diverse writers and adjusting the way one listens for their voices.

From Naomi Iizuka, I learned the simple power of a prompt.

From Erik Ehn, I learned how art can be a radical act of love.

I still strive to live up to the example my teachers helped me envision. And as Mr. Sokoloff would say, "Not quite, Mr. Perry, but it's good for you."

Mark Perry teaches playwriting and play analysis at the University of North Carolina at Chapel Hill and serves as a dramaturg for PlayMakers Repertory Company. In 2002, he began Drama Circle, which is dedicated to using the arts to build community.

www.ingramcontent.com/pod-product-compliance
Lightning Source LLC
LaVergne TN
LVHW091002080826
845145LV00003B/1095